ICE design and practice guide

Coastal defence

Edited by Alan Brampton

Thomas Telford

Published by Thomas Telford Publishing, Thomas Telford Ltd, 1 Heron Quay, London E14 4JD. URL: http://www.thomastelford.com

Distributors for Thomas Telford books are
USA: ASCE Press, 1801 Alexander Bell Drive, Reston, VA 20191-4400, USA
Japan: Maruzen Co. Ltd, Book Department, 310 Nihonbashi 2-chome, Chuo-ku, Tokyo 103
Australia: DA Books and Journals, 648 Whitehorse Road, Mitcham 3132, Victoria

First published 2002

Front cover photo: The shingle barrier beach, Selsey Bill, Sussex

A catalogue record for this book is available from the British Library

ISBN: 0 7277 3005 3

Typeset by Gray Publishing, Tunbridge Wells, Kent
Printed and bound in Great Britain by MPG Books, Bodmin, Cornwall

Coastal defence

ICE design and practice guides

One of the major aims of the Institution of Civil Engineers is to provide its members with opportunities for continuing professional development. One method by which the Institution is achieving this is the production of design and practice guides on topics relevant to the professional activities of its members. The purpose of the guides is to provide an introduction to the main principles and important aspects of the particular subject, and to offer guidance as to appropriate sources of more detailed information.

The Institution has targeted as its principal audience practising civil engineers who are not expert in or familiar with the subject matter. This group includes recently graduated engineers who are undergoing their professional training and more experienced engineers whose work experience has not previously led them into the subject area in any detail. Those professionals who are more familiar with the subject may also find the guides of value as a handy overview or summary of the principal issues.

Where appropriate, the guides will feature checklists to be used as an *aide-mémoire* on major aspects of the subject and will provide, through references and bibliographies, guidance on authoritative, relevant and up-to-date published documents to which reference should be made for reliable and more detailed guidance.

Preface

Civil engineering at the coast has been carried out for thousands of years. Initially, the impetus was provided by the development of harbours and ports, i.e. providing breakwaters and quays. This was followed by the construction of embankments to convert inter-tidal areas to fertile agricultural land. The birth of seaside resorts in the Regency period set new challenges for engineers, for example the provision of promenades and the stabilization of cliffs and beaches to improve the amenity value of the coast. Later the Industrial Revolution, and the development of the railways that often ran along the shore, led to the widespread construction of seawalls to provide level ground along the coastal strip. Development of the coastal zone continues, including for example the construction of power stations, oil refineries and marinas.

As a consequence of this range of activities, many of the most intensively developed areas of the UK, and overseas, lie at or close to the coast. Such areas are of great economic and social value, for example containing industrial, commercial or residential properties as well as high-grade agricultural land. In addition, the coastline often also provides opportunities for tourism as well as, formal and informal recreation.

Apart from these numerous human uses of the coastal zone, it has an intrinsic natural importance, for example providing habitats for a wide range of flora and fauna. In addition, the action of the sea on the edge of the land produces rapid changes in the coastal morphology, revealing the underlying rock strata, causing landslides and reshaping the shoreline, all effects of great interest to geologists. Because of these attributes, parts of the coastline (especially where they have remained undeveloped) have been designated as of national or international importance from a scientific or conservation viewpoint. Sensitive management of these areas is of crucial importance both now and into the future.

The desire to preserve assets in the coastal zone has resulted in the widespread installation of coastal defences, i.e. structures designed to resist the erosion or flooding of land by the sea. This particular branch of civil engineering has a long history in the UK. Although well intended, coastal defence schemes have often resulted in detrimental effects on adjacent stretches of shoreline, or have subsequently required increasingly expensive maintenance or rebuilding. Alternatives to traditional forms of defences, such as seawalls, have therefore been developed to reduce both costs and adverse effects on the surrounding area. In some areas, the need for maintaining existing defences is now being reviewed in strategic reviews of the coastline and its management. The alternative of allowing parts of the coastline to revert to a more natural pattern of behaviour, and dealing with the consequences of its subsequent evolution, may ultimately prove more cost-effective and sustainable than continuing to defend it. In many highly developed areas, however, the protection of people and property from the sea will remain a necessity into the indefinite future, although the type of coastal defences may well change.

The whole task of planning, designing, building and managing coastal defences in a cost-effective, environmentally acceptable and sustainable manner is a complicated undertaking, involving a wide range of skills. Hopefully this introductory guide to the subject will give a flavour of the challenge involved, particularly for civil engineering, which is at the centre of this continuing challenge.

Acknowledgements

This design and practice guide was initiated by the Maritime Board of the Institution of Civil Engineers. The steering group members for the production of this guide were as follows:

Hugh Payne (Chairman)	Welsh Office/National Assembly for Wales
Alan Brampton (Editor)	HR Wallingford Limited
Noel Beech	Posford Haskoning Ltd.
Andy Bradbury	New Forest District Council
Jan Brook	Posford Duvivier Environment/Independent Consultant
Chris Fleming	Halcrow Maritime Ltd
Sian John	CIRIA/Posford Haskoning Ltd
David Richardson	Department of Environment, Food and Rural Affairs, London
Keith Riddell	Babtie Limited
Michael Owen	Independent Consultant
Andrew Usborne	The Environment Agency
Martin Wright	Gwynedd County Council/Independent Consultant

The text for this guide was generated from contributions from the steering group members and the editor.

The Maritime Board is grateful to the contributors and their organizations for their support, and for the funding contribution provided by the Environment Agency. The Board emphasizes that the views expressed in this guide do not necessarily reflect the opinions of the organizations or individual contributors.

The editor gratefully acknowledges the assistance provided by June Taylor of the Institution of Civil Engineers and Maria Stewart of Thomas Telford Limited in the production of this guide, all who have commented on earlier versions of the text and those who have provided photographs and illustrations.

Picture credits.
HR Wallingford Ltd	2, 4–9, 11, 14–22, 25–27
West Dorset DC	23
New Forest DC	24

Contents

1. Introduction

For many centuries, man has developed the coastline and its immediate hinterland for both commercial and cultural reasons. Flat land adjacent to the sea is in great demand for many purposes, including agriculture, ports, roads and railways, power stations and refineries, and residential properties. In many areas, substantial tracts have been reclaimed from the sea to increase the land available for development. A substantial part of the national economy of the UK, and many other countries, is now generated in the coastal zone.

However, the areas of the coastal zone of greatest value, i.e. that on top of low cliffs, reclaimed areas and low-lying coastal plains, are often at greatest risk from the sea. The continuing action of waves and tides, together with the slow increase in global sea level relative to the land, results in the majority of the shorelines around the world suffering recession. Because of this, risks to the developed areas from marine flooding, and erosion of the land itself, increase with time and may be growing faster due to the changing climate. It is widely expected that global warming will cause both acceleration in sea-level rise, and changes in the frequency and intensity of storms, thus altering both wave conditions and tidal surges.

For many centuries, the response to these risks has been to resist the action of the sea by the construction of coastal defences, i.e. structures designed to reduce the risks of erosion or flooding. These range from simple earth embankments to sophisticated civil engineering structures such as tidal barrages. The construction of coastal defences is expensive, and carries the risk of substantial damage to the environment. This is often an important consideration because the coastline often also provides very important habitats for a very wide range of flora and fauna, as well as opportunities for tourism, formal and informal recreation.

In addition, it can be difficult to design and build a structure that will be both effective and long lasting. This guide aims to introduce the reader to the process of considering and, if appropriate, choosing, designing, building and maintaining coastal defences appropriate to a particular situation.

The guide starts with a review of the history of coastal defences in the UK, and of the legal administrative arrangements for their construction. This is followed by a description of the important processes causing changes to the coast, and examples of the commonest types of coastal defences. After this the guide goes on to discuss the information needed to decide whether installing defences is justifiable, and how to choose appropriate types of defence for further consideration. These decisions have to take account of the technical, environmental and economic aspects of any proposed scheme. In the remainder of the report, the issues of detailed design, construction and post-construction activities are explained.

Managing the coastline involves many issues, both technical and non-technical, and it is unlikely that any individual coastal engineer will have sufficient depth of knowledge in all of the disciplines required. In addition to civil engineering, expertise will be required in geology and geomorphology, environmental or ecological science, archaeology, risk analysis and project management. There may also need to be an involvement from oceanographers, marine biologists, information technologists, meteorologists, economists and others.

A considerable body of knowledge and expertise on coastal defence in the UK, and in many other countries, already exists. Much of the knowledge that has gradually been built up over many years has been set down in reference books and technical papers, but research continues apace with new publications appearing regularly. Even against this background, the problems encountered at each site are often unique, and require a carefully tailored solution requiring experienced specialists to achieve cost effective and technically sound coastal defences. Use of general technical guidance documents is no substitute for specialist expertise and site-specific investigation.

2. Coastal defences

2.1 History and background

Human attitudes and responses to coastline change vary considerably around the world. In some areas, for example, it is illegal to erect defences to prevent erosion. Instead threatened assets have either to be abandoned, or moved inland to preserve them, often incurring considerable expense.

Elsewhere, including the UK, there has been a long tradition of preventing flooding and reducing the coastal erosion that leads to shoreline retreat. Planners and politicians have relied on coastal defences to protect, for an indefinite period, a wide range of commercial, industrial, residential and recreational developments in areas at risk. Indeed, the success of past schemes to avoid flooding and erosion has given planners confidence to allow further development close to naturally eroding shorelines, or in areas where the land lies below the level of highest tides.

Many parts of England and Wales are low-lying, reclaimed land. In some areas, the land is below 0 m ODN (which is approximately equal to mean sea level). Figure 1 shows the areas defined by The Environment Agency (1999) as 'Extremely low-lying land' and is taken from a report by the Climate Change Impacts Review Group (1996). The shaded areas rely on flood defences that may be natural, e.g. dunes or shingle ridges, but are mainly man-made. In the long term, such areas are theoretically liable to marine flooding, although this would only occur in the (unlikely) eventuality that all the coastal defences were abandoned.

Background and history of coastal defences in the UK

Coastal defences have been built in the UK at least since the time of the Romans; their flood embankments are recorded, for example, on the Severn Levels in South Wales. Until about 200 years ago, virtually the sole objective of coastal defence was protection of low-lying agricultural land and creation of new, fertile land by enclosing and draining inter-tidal areas. Any substantial buildings were generally located above flood level, or were designed to cope with flooding.

Erosion of the UK coast has caused major loss of land over the centuries, with many villages and several substantial towns lost to the sea. Natural rates of retreat of soft cliffs in Yorkshire, East Anglia and Kent, for example, are typically 12 m/ year, but little was done to prevent this land loss because of the great expense involved. Defences against such erosion started in earnest in the late eighteenth

---

and nineteenth century when sea bathing and walking along the seafront became fashionable. Promenades, i.e. wide, level and solid walkways along the beach crest, were built to facilitate this new recreation and solid walls, adjacent to the beach, were subsequently installed to protect their seaward edges in most cases. Often the works included an element of land 'gain', providing valuable new areas for the developing resorts and offsetting the costs.

At about the same time, defences were also built to protect the growing coastal infrastructure such as roads and railways. The continuing growth of industry, for example commercial harbours, power stations, oil refineries and, more recently, the construction of new sewage treatment works or pumping stations, has also required defences to prevent damage or loss of these developments, especially if they have been built on reclaimed land.

Defences have also been built in response to particular social circumstances at different times in the past. For example, in the 1930s seawalls were built around reclaimed areas as part of an initiative to regenerate the local economy. After World War II, seawalls and other structures were built as part of an initiative to allow better public access to the coastline, and to protect valuable agricultural land at a time when food was rationed. The infamous North Sea surge of January/February 1953, for example, caused widespread damage to coastal defences (see Figure 2) and resulted in major flooding of low-lying coastal towns and villages as well as agricultural land. This event provoked a major programme of renewal and improvement of flood defences.

The 'reclamation' of inter-tidal areas, for commerce or industry, and the construction of new flood banks to protect low-lying land has continued to the present. However, most coastal defence schemes now being carried out are to reduce the risk of flooding of commercial or residential properties, particularly in urban areas where land levels are below that of highest tides. In areas where only a small area of low-grade agricultural land is at risk from the sea, existing defences are not always being renewed; some are being deliberately breached to accommodate the natural processes of coastal recession and create new habitats for wildlife.

Pressures to build and maintain coastal defences today are often even greater than in the past. Increased demand for residential property close to the coastal strip and greater use of the coast for recreation and tourism have led to the creation and expansion of resorts that are major wealth creators. Elsewhere, major industrial investments such as power stations and oil/gas terminals have been built close to the shoreline. Allowing the sea to damage or destroy these developments would usually be politically and economically unacceptable. In recent years, there has also been a desire to protect sites that are important because of their ecological or archaeological attributes, although allowing continued erosion and/or inundation remains important at others, for example sites designated because of their geological, geomorphological or other 'earth science' interest.

It is important to realize, however, that the installation of defences can and often does cause problems elsewhere along the coast. Groynes will retain material on one part of a beach, but often at the cost of depriving another area of sediment. Seawalls will prevent the natural erosion of cliffs that previously supplied sediment to the beaches,

Figure 1 Low-lying land areas
(Climate Change Impacts
Review Group, 1996)

Low-lying land

and also restrict the natural slow landward movement of a shoreline caused by the gradual rise in sea level. Beach levels in the vicinity of defence structures hence become lower and it has often proved necessary to extend defences both along the coast, and downwards, to counter this effect.

The traditional presumption in favour of maintaining existing defences, and extending them where new risks of erosion or flooding arise, is now being seriously reconsidered. Factors such as the environmental damage caused by defences, their sustainability and their great cost are all weighty considerations. Economic evaluation methods have shown that the renewal of some defences is not worthwhile, and has altered plans for others. A consequence of these considerations has been a more rational approach to the evaluation, design and construction of defences.

In particular, greater efforts are now being made to define the risks of erosion or flooding, and to design defences that provide an appropriate level of protection to the land behind them. By such means, the needs and benefits for expensive schemes can

Figure 2   Damage to seawall in 1953 storm surge, Trusthorpe, Lincolnshire

be justified, and priorities established to ensure that the most deserving and urgent cases are dealt with first.

Part of this approach to considering coastal defences involves analysing the coastal changes described in Section 3.3. This will usually involve estimating future erosion or recession of both protected and unprotected coastlines, and calculating the consequences for assets close to the coast. Such predictions rely to a considerable extent on the extrapolation of past changes in the shoreline, although mathematical modelling techniques have proved worthwhile where extrapolation is not appropriate (see Section 7.2).

In addition, the threats posed by extreme wave and tide conditions also need to be evaluated. Where the main reason for coastal defences lies in the risk of flooding, then it is appropriate to calculate the likelihood and consequences of such events. This necessarily leads to an examination of the possible combinations of tide levels and waves that might occur, and the performance of existing defences (natural or man-made) under those conditions (see Section 6.1).

2.2 Coastal defences – who builds them?

Powers and responsibilities for construction of coastal defences vary from country to country. This publication considers such aspects primarily in the context of the situation in the UK; legislation and responsibilities for coastal defence will be different in other countries.

As previously noted, the sea can cause damage to assets, including but not limited to man-made structures, in two main ways. It can flood them, or it can erode away the ground on which they stand. In the UK, defence against these two dangers is distinguished in legislation. The prevention of erosion and encroachment is termed Coast Protection, while the avoidance or control of flooding and inundation is termed Sea Defence. 'Coastal defence' is undertaken to prevent or control such damage and is a convenient term that is used to cover both coast protection and sea defence.

Coastal defence policy is set by the Government and the 'Strategy for Flood and Coastal Defence in England and Wales' (produced by the former Ministry of Agriculture, Fisheries and Food & Welsh Office, 1993) provides a more detailed view of the policy framework. The aim of the policy is to reduce the risks to people and the developed and natural environment from flooding and erosion, through the following steps:

— encouraging the provision of adequate and cost effective flood-warning systems,
— encouraging the provision of technically, economically and environmentally sound and sustainable flood and coastal defence measures, and
— discouraging inappropriate development in areas at risk from flooding or coastal erosion.

The fact that there are two kinds of coastal defence, and three different sets of legislation in England and Wales alone, owes much to the historical development of coastal defence. Sea defence, being primarily for the protection of agricultural land and integral with fluvial flood defence, has long been the province of those responsible for managing rivers. Presently this type of defence tends to be the responsibility of the Environment Agency.

On the other hand, coast protection has always been primarily concerned with the protection of urban centres on the coast, and thus has been the responsibility of the local councils. Consolidation of sea defence and coast protection arrangements has been strongly resisted by the councils who see the provision and maintenance of promenades, seawalls, access steps and the like as an important part of the amenities of their coastline, especially in holiday resorts. The legislation and responsibilities for coastal defence in the UK are briefly outlined in the box below.

Coastal defence legislation in the UK

Coast protection in England, Scotland and Wales may be carried out under the Coast Protection Act (1949) by maritime district or borough councils, or by unitary councils where there is only the one tier of local government. These councils are required to consult over major construction or re-construction schemes with the Environment Agency, neighbouring councils, national conservation organizations (e.g. English Nature), harbour authorities and fisheries bodies. Approvals and/or licences may also be required from various government departments and other bodies who will check, for example, that the proposed scheme is unlikely to cause environmental damage or be a danger to navigation.

The government department with responsibility for administering the Coast Protection Act will give ultimate approval and may also assist financially with a scheme. There can be a relaxation of the consultation requirements when emergency works are necessary. Note, however, that while the Coast Protection Act provides 'permissive' powers, it does **not** impose a duty on those authorities to install coastal defences.

Landowners, railway owners, highway and harbour authorities may also undertake coast protection works. Such bodies must normally consult the relevant coast protection authority before commencement of works.

Sea defence in England and Wales may be undertaken by the Environment Agency, who have overall supervisory powers to protect against flooding, under the Water Resources Act (1991). There is no requirement in that legislation for the Environment Agency to consult with others or to obtain consent from a minister. In practice, though, consultation is required to satisfy environmental and safety legislation and consent from the appropriate government ministry is required to obtain financial assistance.

Sea defence works may also be undertaken by councils or by internal drainage boards, under the Land Drainage Act (1991), and owners may undertake works on their own property. Sea defence works may only be undertaken with the consent of the Environment Agency. In Scotland, the relevant legislation for coastal flood defence is the 1961 Flood Prevention Act (Scotland).

2.3 Coastal zone management

The coastline and the coastal zone, i.e. an area of land and water on either side of the coastline, are very important assets to the UK, as in many other countries. Many people involved in commerce, transport, industry and tourism have the coastal zone as their main focus of activity. In addition, there is increasing pressure on this zone from people wishing to live close to the sea, with related demands for infrastructure to support residential, recreational and tourism developments. Hence there is likely to be a continuing demand for coastal defences, both to replace the ageing stock, and for newly developed areas. However, the remaining undeveloped stretches of coastline are often of great environmental importance, particularly from the viewpoints of biological diversity and landscape value.

The management of the coastal zone is also complicated by the dynamic nature of both the sea and the shoreline. Flooding of low-lying land, and the effects of marine erosion leading to the recession of beaches and cliffs and loss of land, can result in considerable difficulties either in planning new development, or in maintaining existing assets close to the shore. These difficulties are further compounded by the probability of changes in the climate, with a widely predicted increase in sea levels.

Coastal areas are subject to the same planning and political conflicts as other areas. However, some extra management problems arise because of the land/sea divide being a boundary of ownership and legal powers; for example, planning authorities often do not have responsibility for the seabed below the low water mark. Further, there are many authorities/groups, other than those responsible for coastal defences, that have a responsibility for, or an interest in, the coastal zone. Port authorities and conservation bodies are good examples. These many different groups often have very different concerns and priorities regarding the coastline and its management.

It is, therefore, very difficult to carry out coastal management in a practical and cost-effective way, while satisfying everyone. Over the last decade or so, in the UK and elsewhere, these problems have led to the development of coastal zone management. This is an approach to planning aimed at careful and sustainable management of the coastal zone reconciling the many, sometimes-conflicting needs and constraints that exist.

Managing beaches and providing defences against flooding and erosion is just one area of coastal zone management, but the particular one that this guide focuses on. However, it should always be remembered that other initiatives and options for the management of the shoreline, and the wider coastal zone, will need to be considered for each particular situation. For example, relocating assets at risk, or avoiding new developments close to the present-day shoreline may be preferable to coastal defence works, both from the economic and environmental viewpoints.

Further information on coastal zone management in the UK can be obtained from the following publications:

— Department of the Environment (1995 and 1996), for England
— Council for Nature Conservation and the Countryside (1995) for Northern Ireland
— Scottish Office (1996) for Scotland
— Welsh Office (1998) and National Assembly for Wales (1999) for Wales.

This issue is also attracting considerable interest in Europe (e.g. Commission of the European Communities 1992, 1995).

2.4 A strategic approach to coastal defence

A common and often valid criticism of coastal defences is that many have been erected in a piecemeal fashion, sometimes as an emergency response to a particular event, e.g. a cliff fall or a major flood. This has often resulted in further problems elsewhere along the shoreline, and the building of further coastal defence structures. In addition, the need for rapid action has sometimes caused damage to the environment or other interests that could have been avoided if more time had been available for consultations and amendments to the designs.

Because of the difficulties caused by such reactive responses, and in anticipation of the benefits of a longer term and holistic view, a more strategic approach to planning and installing coastal defences is now being adopted. Each stage requires an understanding of coastal processes, coastal defence needs, environmental considerations, planning issues and current and future land use, but at an appropriate level of detail. The assessment of risk is an integral part of the appraisal process at each stage to ensure decisions taken at that time are robust and based on an awareness of the consequences and appropriate mitigation measures. The elements of this approach are illustrated in Table 2.1.

The strategic planning and specific implementation of coastal defence works forms the main subject of this Guide. The remainder of this chapter describes shoreline management plans in more detail.

To assist in the process of preparing shoreline management plans, the coastline of England and Wales has been divided into sediment 'cells' and 'sub-cells' (Figure 3). A similar exercise has also been undertaken for Scotland (Scottish Natural Heritage, 1997). Each cell is defined as a length of shoreline that is relatively self-contained as far as the movement of beach sand and shingle is concerned, so that any interruption

Table 2.1 Stages in the appraisal process

Stage	Shoreline management plans	Strategy plan	Scheme
Aim	To identify policies to reduce risks	To identify appropriate scheme types to implement policies	To identify the nature of works to implement preferred scheme
Delivers	Broad-brush assessment of risks, constraints and opportunities, areas of uncertainty	Preferred approach (i.e. scheme type) including economic and environmental decisions	Comparison of different implementation options for preferred scheme type
Output	Generic policies (e.g. hold the line, advance the line, etc.)	Type of scheme (e.g. beach management, linear defence, setback embankment, etc.)	Type of works (e.g. revetment, seawall, recycling, etc.)

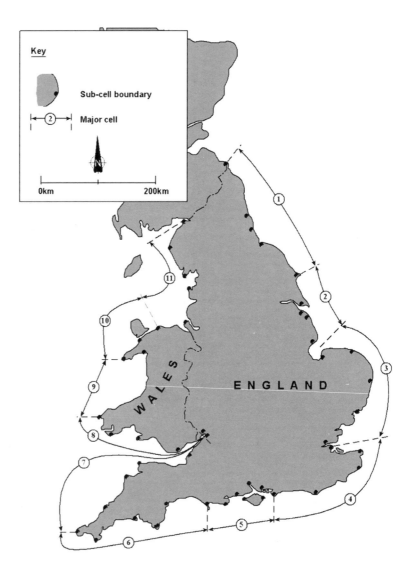

Figure 3 Coastal cells and sub-cells, England and Wales (HR Wallingford, 1993)

Figure 4   Beach accumulation updrift of West Bay harbour, Dorset

Second, most beaches are only thin layers of sediment lying on a solid rock or consolidated clay substrate, often a nearly flat and gently seaward sloping 'shore platform'. The plan shape of a coast is also largely controlled by the topography of the solid rock, for example the headlands between which the beaches are retained. Even the hardest rocks will eventually be eroded by the continual action of waves and tidal currents, while softer rocks such as clay shore-platforms or cliffs of glacial till, erode more rapidly than older harder strata. As the rock is eroded, often accelerated by the abrasive action of the sand and gravel particles moving over its surface, the beaches will also change, generally retreating landwards. Figure 5, for example, shows an exposed chalk shore-platform from which the overlying beach sediment has been removed by storm wave action. While some extra sediment for beaches is produced by the abrasion of the platform, in this case flint nodules, the overall effect will be of lowered beach levels.

Typical problems caused by the long-term changes in open coasts include:

— lowering and steepening of beaches, especially in front of seawalls, as the shore platform is lowered by abrasion, a process accelerated by sea-level rise (see Figure 5)

— over-washing, recession and/or breaching of barrier beaches and dunes, usually by a combination of high tide levels and severe waves (see Figures 6 and 7)

— erosion of cliffs and coastal slopes, with waves eroding their seaward toe, hence 'preparing' for a collapse, e.g. rotational slip or block collapse (see Figure 8).

3.3.2 Estuarial coastline changes

Within estuaries and tidal inlets, wave heights and the forces they create are smaller than on the open coast. Historically many such coastlines have accumulated sediment. This sediment arrives both from the open coast and from inland, borne to the coast by rivers. Salt-tolerant vegetation establishes itself in the upper inter-tidal zone, helping to stabilize the sediment and encouraging further accretion of sediment. Tidal currents play a significant role in transporting sediment and in changing the shape of these coastlines. Fine-grained, cohesive particles of mud and clay usually predominate but sand and shingle bars and banks are frequently present, particularly in the seaward parts of the estuaries.

The morphological development of estuaries and tidal inlets is often unpredictable, both on the local scale (e.g. as a result of the meandering of channels) and on a wider scale, with whole estuaries undergoing long periods of accretion followed by similar periods of erosion. The fundamental causes of these longer-term changes often remain obscure.

Figure 5   Exposed and eroding shore platform, Sheringham, Norfolk

Figure 6   Eroding dunes, Sumburgh, Shetland

Figure 7   Waves overtopping shingle barrier beach, Selsey Bill, Sussex

The combination of deep-water channels and shelter from waves afforded by estuaries has frequently led to the development of ports, power stations and other industry along their shorelines. In addition, advantage was taken of the gradual accretion in estuaries and large areas of the inter-tidal zone have been enclosed and converted

Figure 8   Eroding sandy cliffs, Easton Bavents, Suffolk

into fertile agricultural land. Even at the time of their enclosure, many such areas were below the level of the highest tides. Subsequently, sea level has risen, and the land itself has often consolidated as it was drained, with the consequence that large areas close to estuaries are at risk of inundation, to a substantial depth, either from the sea, from rivers or both. The enclosures were achieved by the erection of flood banks around low-lying areas. These were normally simple clay embankments, built at the landward edge of saltmarshes, where water depths were small even during the highest tides. Later periods of erosion within the estuary have increased water depths, and hence wave heights, at the face of these relatively weak structures, causing damage and sometimes collapse and breaching. To prevent such damage, many of the original embankments have been strengthened, e.g. by armouring their front face, and raising their crest levels, forming a much more permanent and solid defence, although one that, under extreme conditions, may have an uncertain performance.

Where further erosion occurs, and the inter-tidal mud-flats move landwards, then the saltmarsh area in front of the defences narrows and sometimes disappears completely. Not only does this allow greater wave action on the flood banks, but also the loss of a valuable ecological habitat is a major environmental concern. This phenomenon is called 'coastal squeeze'; it is often argued that was it not for the defences the estuary would widen, and adjust to a new stability, with new saltmarsh areas developing further landwards.

Methods for intervening and controlling estuarine morphology changes are less well developed than for open coastlines. There are few methods, for example for protecting or restoring saltmarsh that have proved successful (Environment Agency, 1996). Until better methods have been developed for predicting changes, either as a result of natural processes or human intervention, then the effects and performance of defences against erosion or flooding in estuarine areas will remain difficult to determine in advance.

4. Review of coastal defence techniques

4.1 Introduction

This chapter describes the most common types of coastal defences that have been used in the UK and elsewhere around the world. Most of these defences have been developed and refined for installation on wave-dominated shorelines. Such coasts typically have beaches of sand, less frequently of shingle, and the interactions between defence structures and these beaches is a crucial factor both in their effectiveness and in longevity. Over the last 20–30 years, there has been a widespread change in views on the types of defence that are most cost-effective and acceptable from an environmental viewpoint. For example, near-vertical impermeable seawalls were once highly rated since they can provide a high standard of protection at low cost. However, they have also tended to adversely affect beaches and therefore require periodic extension or re-building. Defences based on enlarging and maintaining beaches are now popular. Although not necessarily a permanent solution to erosion or flooding problems, they can offer a range of environmental and economic advantages.

The most appropriate type of defence in any location, however, should not be prejudged. Decisions have to be made bearing in mind both the particular characteristics of the site and the standard of defence that is appropriate. In the UK, coastal defence design often includes extending, repairing or renewing existing structures. It is rare to have to design schemes where no coastal defence structures already exist.

In the following, the main advantages and disadvantages of the numerous defence types are summarized as an aid to the identification of suitable options. It is important to point out that it is rare for any single type of defence to be installed on its own; a combination of techniques often provides the best solution.

Finally, it is important to realize that special consideration should be given to coastlines with cliffs, sand dunes and especially those within estuaries. Separate sections of this chapter have been provided to indicate the extra or alternative methods of coastal defence in these situations.

4.2 Linear defences

4.2.1 Introduction

'Linear defences', for example seawalls, are the most obvious form of coastal defence. They consist of techniques applied either directly along the shoreline, or close by and parallel to it, to strengthen or protect the immediate area from storm attack. More knowledge and experience has been acquired regarding these than any other form of defence. Nevertheless, a 'scientific' approach to their design and construction has only been developed over the last century, and this has gone hand-in-hand with an appreciation that such an installation is generally only one element in an overall coastal management plan.

In order to design linear defences, whether embankments, revetments or seawalls, information is needed on:

— the tidal levels and wave conditions it needs to withstand
— the levels of the beaches and/or the shore platform on which it is to be built, and
— the geotechnical characteristics of the ground conditions.

The design of the defence will need to provide satisfactory performance under four headings, namely overtopping, stability, durability and environmental effects. These aspects are now considered in turn.

4.2.1.1 Overtopping. In order to perform its main function, a defence needs to prevent, or reduce to acceptable levels, the amount of water that passes over it even in severe conditions, i.e. large waves occurring at times of high tidal levels. The capacity of the defence to prevent overtopping is mainly dependent on the following parameters:

— the defence height, slope, berms and any special features such as a wave return wall
— the roughness and permeability of the front face of the defence
— the level and slope of the foreshore fronting the defence.

4.2.1.2 Stability. A coastal defence structure must be able to withstand the forces imposed on it. Principally these are the pressures and overturning moments caused by the action of waves and tides. In addition, it must withstand both steady and transient forces within and beneath the structure. These various forces and pressures depend on the parameters that influence overtopping rates, as listed above, but also on:

— the size and weight of the structural elements of the defence
— the strength of the interconnections between those elements
— permissible foundation pressures, and
— drainage arrangements and permeability.

4.2.1.3 Durability. The durability of a defence will depend on the same parameters that influence its stability, but also on other parameters which affect the long-term, often gradual, changes in its structure, namely:

— quality of materials used, and of initial construction
— harshness of environment, controlling mechanical and chemical abrasion rates
— long-term beach and foreshore movements, that can lead to undermining of its front face
— maintenance arrangements, i.e. planning, monitoring and execution.

More on these matters is presented in Chapter 7.

4.2.1.4 Environmental effects. The effects that a coastal defence will have on the environment, whether human or natural, are discussed in more detail in Section 6.3. However, for linear defences the key issues are normally the effects on:

— access, amenity, aesthetics and public safety
— beach and foreshore levels, both in front of the defence and along adjacent stretches of coast
— heritage interests (natural and cultural), for example protecting eroding cliffs or historic monuments.

Having discussed the generalities of linear defences, it is now convenient to describe the three most common forms, namely embankments, revetments and seawalls. Occasionally other types of linear defence are encountered, for example 'palisades' and 'breastworks', and these have to be considered and designed on an individual, case-by-case basis.

4.2.2 Embankments

Flood embankments, often called dykes or bunds, are constructed to prevent inundation of low-lying land by high sea levels caused by extreme tides, surges and/or storm activity. Where land is reclaimed from the sea, banks are almost always needed to protect it against flooding by high tides several times each year. In most cases, such reclaimed areas are protected by simple earth or clay embankments.

Earth banks are normally the cheapest forms of linear defence against high water levels, provided suitable materials are available locally and that the value of the strip of land they are built on is not a significant factor in decision making. They must be designed in accordance with good geotechnical practice to provide stability at times of high tidal levels and also when beaches in front of them are lowered, for example by persistent wave action. Surprisingly, water-tightness is not generally an over-riding consideration. It is important that the structure has good internal stability under the hydraulic gradients that can occur. Some leakage of water through the embankment during the time when tidal levels are high will not then cause the damage that would otherwise occur. Migration of fines leading to leaching failure is the major reason for dyke failure and adherence to maximum hydraulic gradient criteria will generally mean that flow rates will not be so high as to necessitate complicated arrangements for draining their rear face.

Initially, the only protection to the surface of earth banks is grass and other natural vegetation, although the crest of the embankment may be lightly armoured, e.g. by asphalt or shingle, to allow access along it. Such protection is unlikely to resist significant wave attack, although moderate overtopping may be adequately withstood. If embankments are used in regions where large waves can occur, more protection is needed. One alternative is to use some type of armouring, particularly on their front face, for example concrete slabs or asphalt. This turns the 'embankment' into a 'revetment', as described in the following section.

Alternatively the incident wave heights may be reduced, for example by the use of breakwaters or by encouraging an increase in foreshore levels. Often, however, the simplest means of achieving this protection is to build the embankment further inland so that its toe is in shallow water, even during high tides, and is hence only exposed to very modest wave action. This method has been employed very successfully on the East Coast and in Somerset, where an embankment is built perhaps 50–100 m inland from the mean high water mark. The intervening area is usually vegetated, and of

Figure 9   Damage to rear face of clay embankment

shallow slope, forming a natural 'berm' at the base of the embankment. The length, level and roughness of this berm then attenuate wave action before it reaches the embankment, reducing both the impact forces and run-up on its face.

Attention must also be paid to the rear face of embankments, for example preventing or repairing damage caused by grazing or burrowing animals. Water overtopping the crest of an embankment and flowing down its rear face, assisted by gravity, can cause serious damage (Figure 9) and is another significant cause of the failure of this type of coastal defence.

4.2.3 Revetments

Protecting soft cliffs and slopes, clay or earth embankments and old marine structures from wave impact forces is generally accomplished by applying some form of revetment. Many new seawalls are more accurately termed revetments since they consist of an embankment core covered by a protective surface layer. A revetment may be either *rigid* or *flexible*, depending on the materials used for its construction.

A flexible revetment will allow for some limited degree of deformation due to settlement of the underlying material, without damage to its outer face (McConnell, 1998).

The main types of revetment commonly used for coastal defences are:

— rock armour and substitutes
— concrete blocks (often inter-connected)
— gabions
— asphaltic blankets
— earth reinforcement.

4.2.3.1 Rock armour and substitutes. Rock armour is probably now the most common form of revetment used in the UK. The availability of appropriate sizes of rock used to be problematic in some areas, leading to wide regional variations in price. This is no longer the case, as more quarries are producing armour-stone, although much of the rock armour used in the UK originates in Scandinavia and France. Where it proves too expensive to obtain large enough rock, substitutes such as concrete cubes, Tetrapods, Dolosse or other patented or specially designed units are sometimes used. These perform the same function as rock. Their shape often allows greater inter-locking of the armour units than can be achieved using quarried rock, so reducing the weight of each unit.

Rock is primarily sized for its resistance to displacement by wave action, and in this regard is substantially more effective as a graded material than when it is of uniform size. Various formulae exist for the determination of rock size capable of withstanding wave attack of specified severity (generally described by height and period parameters) for a given duration.

A second important consideration is of the rock armour's function as a 'blanket' to retain smaller sized material placed beneath it. Rock revetments are built using layers of different sized material, with the finest forming a central 'core', which is then protected by layers of rock of increasing size and weight. To ensure that the finer material is not disturbed and lost through the coarser, strict rules apply as to the rock sizes in the overlying layer compared to those in the underlying material. For this reason, rock revetments are often of two or three layer construction and may include a suitable geotextile to retain the core material or sub-soil. The 'Manual on the use of rock in coastal and shoreline engineering' (CIRIA/CUR, 1991) gives complete guidance on design and construction using rock.

Rock is often favoured for revetment armouring because it has the following advantages:

— the roughness and permeability both help reduce wave run-up and overtopping
— wave reflection is reduced, in turn reducing beach scour at its toe, perhaps even promoting accretion
— the structure will usually have some capacity for 'self-healing' after damage by wave action
— this last attribute also means that rock revetments are unlikely to suddenly collapse or breach, i.e. they typically fail more gradually than a seawall that may collapse without warning
— the rock will often provide a 'niche' habitat colonized by shellfish, and algae hence attracting fish and wading birds.

The usual disadvantages are the possible dangers to pedestrians or beach users, who may be injured clambering over the structure, and its visual aspect, which can be out of character with the surrounding area. If the whole structure is not regularly submerged at high tidal levels, there can also be a problem with rats living in the interstices of the revetment.

The following points may be considered as paramount when considering the suitability and the design of a rock revetment:

— rock size and grading (for a given geometry, i.e. slope and crest height)
  • resistance to wave action
  • effect on run-up and overtopping
  • likely effects on foreshore
  • public safety and amenity considerations
— necessity for filtration and foundation stability
— rock material specification
  • durability
  • availability
  • cost
  • method of delivery.

Rock of smaller size can be incorporated into gabion mattresses or grouted with bituminous or asphaltic material (see McConnell, 1998) to provide an alternative type of revetment.

4.2.3.2 Concrete blocks. Concrete blocks come in a variety of shapes and sizes, either as single units, or interconnected, i.e. 'cable-tied' and supplied in the form of a flexible 'mattress'. Each block in a cable-tied system may weigh as little as a few kilograms, while the single units that rely on friction or interlocking shapes for stability may weigh more than 100 kg. Often the blocks are of proprietary or patented design, hence subject to royalty payments. Concrete block systems are usually placed as a single layer over a prepared slope of finer rock or gravel, with that under-layer often placed on a geotextile filter. Generally, the blocks are laid to produce a plane, sloping face to the revetment and, depending on the type of units used, the face may be smooth or rough, permeable or impermeable.

Block systems, due to their regular nature, are subject to progressive failure should some damage occur. The removal of one block (or failure of one cable or tendon) is likely to adversely affect the stability of adjacent blocks by allowing water pressures to be exerted directly underneath the blocks. For this reason, concrete block revetments are often divided into sections by panel beams running the full height of the slope. Design parameters for these systems have generally been established by physical model testing and design must be carried out by reference to the appropriate published results (see McConnell, 1998). These systems may suffer sudden, catastrophic failure when the wave forces exceed a certain threshold. Examples of concrete block systems include:

— steps and large rectangular slabs: stable by self-weight
— concrete tiles (rectangular or hexagonal): generally lightweight units, jointed with bitumen, and used in mild wave environments
— Essex blocks, T-lock, Dytap, Basaltine, etc.: these rely on mechanical interlock, and sometimes grouting as well, to achieve greater stability.
— Armourflex, Petraflex, etc.: cable-tied systems, produced in the form of mattresses

— Cob, Shed, Seabee, Diode units, etc.: large hollow concrete blocks designed to dissipate wave energy.

With the exception of the hollow block systems, all of these will produce a defence structure with a seaward face that is hydraulically smooth (or nearly so), that is compatible with access requirements as well as leisure and amenity interests. This is at the expense of higher run-up levels than on a rock revetment, a greater effect on the foreshore and adjacent areas and an often less harmonious blend with the natural environment. Dependent on location and site-specific conditions, these systems can compete in price with rock. Once such systems have been damaged, usually either by wave impact forces that displace blocks, or by undermining of their seaward face causing wash-out of the underlying material, repairing them is more difficult than rock revetments.

4.2.3.3 Gabions. Gabions are wire baskets usually filled with stones, cobbles or small rock, but sometimes with concrete blocks such as old kerbstones. They are best considered using the guidance to be found in manufacturer's literature and are generally only suitable in areas where abrasion is low due to the propensity of the steel or plastic wires to abrade, corrode and fail. Common causes of failure include:

— abrasion by beach material, especially shingle
— the breaking up and removal of the material used to fill them, again leading to abrasion of the wires, and
— damage caused by beach users walking over them.

They can be placed either as a near-vertical wall in front of eroding cliffs or dunes, or as a sloping revetment, when their permeability helps to limit wave run-up and overtopping. In an open-coast situation, i.e. where there is significant wave action, gabions are likely to need repair or replacement within 10 years of placement, sometimes sooner.

4.2.3.4 Asphaltic blankets. The use of asphalt in the hydraulic environment has been most developed by the Dutch for the protection of dykes and river channel banks (see Rijkswaterstaat, 1985) and a few such systems have been used in the UK. The asphalt blankets generally rely on preventing hydrodynamic pressures reaching the back of the membrane and possessing sufficient continuity and flexibility to resist the forces acting on the seaward face. They may also be very much thinner than equivalent rock or concrete block constructions. Their impermeability is generally achieved by specifying asphaltic concrete, which is an overfilled mix with self-healing properties when over-stressed.

An alternative permeable material with similar qualities of flexibility and with some claim to energy dissipation and reduced run-up is known as open-stone-asphalt (see McConnell, 1998). It is applied in a much greater thickness in order to achieve sufficient strength. This material consists of single-size stone bound together with an optimally designed asphaltic mix that merely coats every stone without filling the voids.

4.2.3.5 Earth reinforcement. Techniques of earth reinforcement are generally considered as slope stabilization (see Section 4.6) but certain methods involving the use of heavy (usually woven) geotextiles merit inclusion as revetment systems in their own right. Bag-work laid at a slope has long been used as a temporary form of protection. With the advent of modern geotextiles, very large bags laid to a three-dimensional pattern can now offer substantial life expectancy in moderate environments at very low cost. They are typically filled with beach sand *in situ*. Such constructions can be used in the first stages of dune rehabilitation programmes, which may take many years to reach their full effectiveness and provide adequate reassurance against the risk of flooding. The geotextile bags, however, can be easily damaged, for example by vandalism, and hence have to be used with discretion.

4.2.4 Seawalls

In some cases the distinction between revetments and seawalls is not clear-cut, with different people using different terminology. Seawalls, however, typically have the following features:

— construction is of concrete, either pre-cast or poured *in situ*, or of masonry
— a beam along the toe of its seaward face, often supported on piles
— the seaward face is usually solid, e.g. of concrete or stone, and often not a simple plane slope
— it has a rear wall that contributes to the strength of the overall structure
— the crest is also part of the structure and is often designed and used both as an access route and an amenity.

Modern seawalls usually have sloping front faces, like revetments, but often have breaks in the slope and details such as steps (see Figure 10). These features are usually included:

— to dissipate wave energy, and hence reduce overtopping
— to reduce problems of beach lowering at the seawall toe

Figure 10   Seawall with beach recharge operations

— for aesthetic reasons
— to provide good access and an amenity for beach users.

Necessarily, however, this increases the volume of construction materials used, and results in the seawall extending further down the beach profile.

Many vertical and near-vertical seawalls were constructed in UK in the past and their refurbishment or replacement or other special circumstances may still necessitate their consideration today. These special circumstances may include:

— the close proximity of property to be protected
— the absence of beach and nearness of deep water
— the desire for boat moorings or other water access and
— the need to protect existing near-vertical features such as cliffs.

In some countries, vertical seawalls are still regarded as the most suitable forms of coastal defence, because of these factors.

The overtopping performance of a seawall mainly depends on its cross-sectional profile and its roughness, as mentioned above. Often a 'wave return wall' is added at the crest of the seaward face, i.e. a concrete or masonry wall typically 0.5−1.5 m high with a vertical or concave seaward face designed to reflect waves seaward and prevent them overtopping the crest of the wall. The acceptable limit for overtopping at the design standard is governed by public safety considerations, the acceptance potential of the cliff or other natural feature behind the wall, potential damage to property, stability considerations of the rear slope of the wall and flooding implications.

Calculating overtopping discharges for simple types of embankment or seawall can be carried out using numerical methods. Most such methods are empirical, i.e. based on analysis of laboratory test results, but modern models that simulate the wave motions in shallow water up to and on the seawall are also now being employed. Many designs, however, are non-standard and may require physical model testing to assess their performance accurately. Artificial roughness, in the form of rock or concrete protuberances in addition to wave return walls, are often added to basic seawall designs to reduce overtopping during extreme wave and tidal conditions. Further details on the design of seawalls to achieve a desired level of protection against overtopping can be found in (BS6349 Part 1).

The over-riding acceptability criterion for a vertical seawall is its stability. This is achieved by its mass for concrete or masonry 'gravity' structures, or by its depth of penetration and bending strength for timber breastworks or steel sheet pile walls. All of these structures are very sensitive to the level of the foreshore in front of the wall. Unfortunately, due to their highly reflective nature, vertical walls can have a pronounced effect on the immediate foreshore leading to the development of deep scour holes and sometimes to the complete loss of beach.

Concrete is very often the material of choice for seawall construction and its use in the marine environment is subject to special consideration (see for example BS6349 Part 1, *Concrete in Coastal Structures*, edited by R.T. Allen, Thomas Telford, London). For example, the inclusion of steel reinforcement will provide extra strength, but where abrasion reduces the depth of coverage of the reinforcement elements, then the subsequent problems of corrosion can lead to significant weakening of the structure. There is little doubt that significant problems are faced when placing *in situ* concrete

4.5.1 Wind fencing

A variety of methods have been used to reduce the wind-induced shear stresses on the surface of dunes, thus encouraging the deposition of sand. Fences on the seaward face or toe of dunes often only last for a short time, before being damaged or removed entirely by severe storms. Consequently, they are normally built of cheap materials such as brushwood, although plastic mesh has also been successfully used, especially in less vulnerable areas.

4.5.2 Planting of dune-binding grasses

Dunes are normally stabilized by specialized species of grass (e.g. Sand Couch, Marram Grass and Sea Lyme in the UK) which thrive in the unusual ecological niche of the upper part of sand beaches and dune faces. They are both salt- and drought-tolerant and colonize fresh deposits of wind-blown sand, helping to reduce wind speeds over the ground surface, and increasing the soil strength. Propagating and planting these grasses in suitable locations is a good method of improving dune stability and enhancing the environment.

4.5.3 Surface stabilization

In areas severely affected by surface erosion due to wind action (deflation), or where it has been necessary to remove dunes temporarily (e.g. to install a pipeline), the above two methods of restoring dunes may not be sufficiently effective. A number of methods of protecting the surface of dunes have been employed, including covering the ground with fishing nets, coir matting, straw 'blankets' (thatching), or even stabilizing affected areas with a bituminous spray, which later breaks up as vegetation beneath it germinates and grows through it. It is important to ensure that the long-term effects on the environment of such techniques are carefully thought through. Materials that are biodegradable, for example, may be preferred.

4.5.4 Control of pedestrians and grazing animals

Deflation, i.e. the erosion of dunes by winds, often starts in small areas where vegetation has been damaged by trampling or grazing. Controlling the numbers of animals within an area of dunes by fencing (for agricultural animals and people), and by shooting or trapping (for rabbits) is often an effective measure. Pedestrians also need to be managed by installing boardwalks and advisory notices (see Figure 13). Off-road vehicles and motorcycles can be particularly damaging, and need to be prevented from reaching vegetated dunes.

4.6 Estuarial coastal defences

Some coastal defence structures in estuaries, such as revetments, are very similar to those used on the open coast. However, the fine-grained cohesive sediments, i.e. mud and clay, found in estuaries mean that other types of defence, such as beach management, are not applicable, or have not been developed to the same extent. However, the problems arising from erosion and flooding along the shorelines of estuaries should not be regarded as unimportant. Many important commercial, industrial and agricultural areas are at risk from such events. Two techniques specifically used in estuaries are worth mentioning, as described below.

4.6.1 Surge and tidal barriers

Several barrage schemes have been completed, and others are under consideration, around the coastline of the UK and elsewhere in the world. Whether these structures are called barriers, barrages or sometimes weirs, they are all designed to modify, or in some cases totally prevent, the progression of the tide up an estuary or inlet. In this

Figure 13   Pedestrian management over coastal dunes

report we are principally concerned with 'surge protection barriers' whose task is to limit the maximum tidal level upstream of it. The primary example in the UK is the Thames Barrier. Unlike permanent barrages, these barriers are movable and are only operated when necessary. At other times, they are designed to have minimal effect on the existing propagation of the tide. Hence they minimize disruption to navigation, to tidal flows and to the natural processes and environments of the area within which they are set. A review of such barriers, explaining the important issues and giving many examples, has recently been published (Burt & Rees, 2001).

The requirement for such structures to be movable involves large-scale mechanical engineering. Both the supporting structure and the moving components, such as gates, have to be on a substantial scale even across a small tidal inlet or estuary mouth. As a consequence, the initial construction cost and subsequent maintenance commitment are both large, even in comparison with conventional coastal engineering works. The length of shoreline protected, and the assets lying to the landward of it, must both be large to justify such a defence option. Because of this, and the considerable environmental issues involved in any large-scale engineering projects in estuaries, any proposal to erect a surge barrier will need considerable study and evaluation.

There are a number of issues that have to be considered during the design of a surge barrier. These include the following.

4.6.1.1 The impact of its closure on the area downstream. The tidal 'wave' will reflect from its front face, and thus increase tidal levels further seaward. This may require a strengthening and raising of flood defences downstream.

4.6.1.2 Real-time forecasting of tidal levels and surges. A considerable investment in the accurate prediction of high tidal levels will be required, not least because a considerable time is needed to close a large barrier, and early warning has to be given to those navigating in the area. Over-caution may lead to closing the barrier too often, causing inconvenience and perhaps increasing the impacts on the morphology of the estuary. Over-optimism may lead to flooding that could have been prevented by operating the barrier.

4.6.1.3 Impacts on the morphology of the estuary. Although barriers that only close occasionally may not seem likely to have much effect on the long-term patterns of sediment transport and morphological change, these issues always should be considered. As sea levels rise, barriers will need to be operated more frequently, and this too needs to be taken into account. Where such changes are likely to occur, for example changing the width of inter-tidal areas, then there may be consequential effects on the wider environment, particularly on the ecology of the area.

It is likely that all such schemes will require extensive data collection exercises, numerical modelling studies to calculate the effects on tidal flows, sediment transport and morphological change (i.e. siltation and erosion) and exhaustive environmental assessments. Nevertheless, the impacts and costs of a barrier may be less than wide-scale improvement of flood defences along the shorelines further upstream.

4.6.2 Saltmarsh management

Many estuaries and tidal inlets have saltmarsh around their edges. These areas are where sediment has been deposited and subsequently colonized by 'halophytes', i.e. salt-tolerant species of plant. The vegetation both stabilizes the accumulated sediment, by reducing the stresses caused by waves and tidal currents, and helps further sediment settle in amongst the plants. Saltmarsh forms in the upper part of the inter-tidal zone, typically from above mean high water neaps to about that of the highest tidal level. Where the tidal range is large, the saltmarsh can be wide and it then acts as an effective natural coastal defence, greatly reducing the height of waves as they travel over it. Where a saltmarsh fronts a flood embankment, and this is often the case, then it serves a dual purpose, both protecting the vulnerable toe of the defence and reducing wave action on it. This reduces the need for reinforcement or armouring of the embankment and the volume of water that overtops it during a storm. Because of this, the maintenance of saltmarsh areas is a legitimate component of coastal defence management in estuaries.

In much of southern and eastern England, there has been a wide-scale problem of erosion of mud flats and saltmarsh over the last few decades. This has been detrimental to the flood defences, often provoking major expense in armouring them and raising their crest to retain a satisfactory standard of protection. In some areas, this expense has not been justifiable because of the low value of the land at risk from flooding. Alternative, less expensive methods of flood defence have therefore been sought, the most common of which is saltmarsh management.

A number of techniques have been used to protect eroding saltmarsh and/or to encourage its re-establishment in areas from which it has been lost. These are based on the idea of reducing the strength of the waves and tidal currents over and/or in front of the saltmarsh, thus encouraging deposition of silt as a first step to forming new saltmarsh (Environment Agency, 1996). This approach to managing coastal defences also has the advantage that, if successful, it will extend and enhance the important ecological habitat that saltmarsh provides.

There has been a considerable degree of experimentation, and the techniques for protecting saltmarsh are certainly less well established than those used for sandy beaches and dunes. The following types are the most commonly used.

4.6.2.1 Sedimentation fences. These are usually built of brushwood and arranged as a grid on mud flats fronting the eroding seaward edge of a saltmarsh. They allow some flow of water through them, but reduce both waves and current speeds so that sediment deposited within them settles on the seabed.

4.6.2.2 Offshore breakwaters. At a number of locations in Essex, small barges have been towed into position in front of saltmarshes and then 'grounded' by filling them with sand and water. This is essentially the same concept as the use of offshore breakwaters as beach control structures (see Section 4.4). Figure 14 shows a site in Essex where both sedimentation fences and offshore breakwaters (barges) have been installed.

Figure 14   Saltmarsh management schemes, Essex

4.6.2.3 Artificial near-shore banks. In some estuaries, there are natural banks of sand or gravel, called 'cheniers', which have healthy areas of saltmarsh in their lee. This has encouraged the idea of placing sand and gravel as artificial banks on the mud flats in front of eroding saltmarshes. This method has been used at several sites where suitable sediment was available at low cost, as a by-product of dredging in harbours or their approach channels (HR Wallingford, 2001).

4.6.2.4 Other methods. Other techniques that have been attempted have included armouring the eroding face of a saltmarsh with rock, installing artificial seaweed and using mud dredged from navigation channels to recharge eroding areas.

It is fair to say that none of the techniques used has always been successful. Indeed, there have been more failures than successes in saltmarsh management so far, probably because in most cases the erosion of saltmarsh is a symptom of a much larger erosion problem affecting an estuary or tidal inlet as a whole.

4.7 Cliff stabilization

Where coastal defences are installed to protect a cliff or other coastal slope, it may be necessary to consider further works to prevent landslides, which could threaten not only the defences but also property on or above the slope. The main objective is stabilization and prevention of movement. It generally requires one or more of the following techniques (see Brunsden & Prior, 1984, Bromhead, 1986, or Hutchinson, 2001, for further details):

— reducing porewater pressures in slopes by surface or sub-surface drainage
— reducing de-stabilizing forces by re-profiling slopes (including old landslides)
— increasing stability by adding weight to the toe of the slope or increasing the shear resistance along the failure surface
— supporting unstable areas by building retaining structures, or
— preventing or reducing the erosion (e.g. by freeze/thaw, wind) of the surface of coastal slopes.

The appropriateness of these various techniques will vary depending on the geo-technical properties of the land mass under consideration, on financial constraints, and on the environmental impacts that may result from such stabilization procedures. The design of safe and cost-efficient stabilization measures can generally only be achieved by a thorough and detailed investigation of the slope, and this is an area where specialist expertise will often be needed. For example, incorrect installation of drainage work or incautious placement of fill material can reduce the stability of slopes. Further information on this subject is given in Lee & Clark (in press).

The most common techniques are briefly described below.

4.7.1 Drainage

Cost-effective slope drainage measures will depend on the size, depth and mechanism of failure of a slope, the types of soil/rock and their permeability. Where surface run-off is the predominant form of natural slope drainage, for example, then surface/shallow drains with surface erosion control techniques are likely to be the most appropriate techniques.

A wide variety of sub-surface drainage methods have been employed (Bromhead, 1986). They can be expensive to install and require considerable expertise in their design and construction; as a result they may only be affordable for situations where a landslide would cause major damage. The potential long-term reduction in the efficiency of drainage systems, by clogging, also needs to be considered. Schemes should be monitored with a view to remedial works as necessary.

4.7.2 Slope re-profiling

Flattening the overall gradient of a coastal slope is often the most efficient method of increasing its stability. However this may immediately lead to the loss of property on a cliff-top, and hence remove the benefit of the works being carried out. Other options include 'toe-weighting' where material is imported and placed at the base of a slope, excavating and replacing landslide debris with granular rock, and incorporating 'benches' or 'terraces' into the slope, which can reduce weathering and help in the control of surface water run-off. Figure 15 shows an example of the use of both drainage and terracing to help stabilize clay cliffs in Dorset.

4.7.3 Soil reinforcement

A number of techniques are available that improve the resistance of soils to failure and deformation. These include:

— piling and soil nailing
— shear keys
— grouting, and chemical injection including lime stabilization.

Figure 15 Terracing and drainage of 'soft rock' cliffs in Dorset

Further reading on data management and sharing can be found in the MUSEC report (CIRIA, 2000).

5.2.2 Collection of data on physical processes and characteristics

5.2.2.1 Geology and geotechnics. The collection of this type of data helps to understand the geological foundation and geomorphological evolution of the coast, beach and foreshore. The solid geology of a coastal area, including the seabed, forms a framework within which the waves and tides act, redistributing the mobile sediments on beaches and the seabed.

Geological plans and geomorphological mapping may only be necessary at the shoreline management plan stage but, when considering the design of a coastal defence structure, further investigation of a site may include:

— a desk study to locate and review existing information, and to identify specific requirements, e.g. for foundations
— site surveys, e.g. trial pits, shell/auger drilling, cone penetration tests, core drilling, shallow seismic surveys.

5.2.2.2 Coastal morphology. A carefully planned programme for collecting information on coastal morphology is invaluable if past and present changes are to be understood and future changes predicted. Such a programme will include some of the following techniques:

— analysis of historical maps of shoreline/cliff top positions
— beach profiling (including any defences or dunes at the beach crest)
— beach plan shape surveys, especially in areas with complicated contours, e.g. behind offshore breakwaters
— surveys locating the seaward edge of dunes, cliffs or, in estuaries, of saltmarshes
— beach sediment sampling and analysis
— fixed aspect photographs (e.g. taken looking along the shoreline from chosen 'standard' locations)
— aerial photographs, both vertical and oblique.

It should be noted that it will take several years of monitoring to identify any long-term trends in beach morphology, due to the inevitable variations in wave conditions from year to year. It is also important to have information on seasonal, and ideally even shorter-term, changes in beach profile to assist in the design of defences. Vertical changes of beach level of up to 2 m during a single storm are not unusual and will have a significant effect on wave action on defences at the beach crest.

5.2.2.3 Nearshore seabed. There are two main aspects of interest.

1. Bathymetry, i.e. the underwater morphology of the seabed, can be established by analysis of navigation charts and near-shore hydrographic surveying. Changes in morphology, especially where there are channels and sandbanks close inshore, can have a significant impact on the evolution of the shoreline and beaches.

2. Seabed sediments, the spatial distribution and particle sizes of sediments on the near-shore seabed can give guidance on possible gains and losses of beach sediments. Data can be obtained on both the surface and sub-surface sediments using both direct sampling and remote sensing techniques, with, for example, the type and size of bedforms providing information on sediment transport directions and rates.

5.2.2.4 Waves, winds and tides. Knowledge of the waves and tides that affect a coastline, altering its beaches and morphology, is essential to understand past changes and for assessing the shoreline's future evolution.

— Weather records, particularly measurements of winds, are available from meteorological archives or from numerical models of the atmosphere. These can be used, in combination with wave measurements and numerical models of wave generation, to predict wave conditions offshore from a coastline.

— In the UK, tide level records are available from approximately 40 class A gauges and a further 60 privately owned gauges. In many cases, the main interest is the prediction of highest tidal levels, for use when designing the crest level of coastal defences. For this purpose, summaries of predicted extreme tidal levels have recently been updated for many locations around the coast of England and Wales, and reported, in 1997, by Dixon and Tawn. The approach employed in this report tries to cover the whole country in a consistent and continuous way, focussing particularly on the high extreme values. However, the search for measured tidal data used in the report was not exhaustive, being confined to A-Class gauge data and earlier annual maxima from a number of other sites. Therefore, this report should not be used as a substitute for a thorough site-specific study, but as an input to such a study. Additional years of data and/or information from non-A-Class gauges, including anecdotal data and previous studies, are often available for site-specific studies. The report by Dixon and Tawn therefore recommends that other sources of data be reviewed. In particular, it makes the point that if the 1-year value can be determined accurately from additional local data, that this should be used, together with the rate of increase with return period from the report to provide a better estimate of extreme tidal levels at the specific location.

— Direct measurements of wave conditions are much less readily available. Measurements around the UK coast, for example, are generally sparse. In 1991, the available information was used to produce a wave 'atlas' (Draper, 1991) which gives an approximate guide to the intensity of wave conditions at different times of the year. Catalogues indicating where wave measurements have been made do exist, for example for the coasts of England and Wales (Harford, 1998), although not all the wave measurements are necessarily available, as many are collected for commercial purposes and may only be obtained at some cost. Information for some other countries can be located on the Internet, especially where there are national wave recording networks (for example the work of NOAA in the USA). However, in general the chances of locating data that is directly useful for any particular site where defences are being considered remain slim.

— In deep water, well offshore, there is now a growing amount of information on wave conditions gathered by satellites. These measurements are made by altimeters, and results obtained by gauging the roughness of the sea surface using the variation on the measurements of the height of the instrument above the sea. Further processing of the signal can now provide estimates of the surface wavelength (and hence allow the wave period to be estimated). However, such measurements are not accurate close to the shoreline, and repeat visits of the satellite to the same point over the sea can be many days apart.

— Since the advent of numerical wave forecasting models, e.g. the Meteorological Office Fine Mesh Wave Model (1986), reasonably accurate information on deep-water wave conditions is available for most of the world, and at finer resolution around the British Isles. This 'synthetic' wave data also includes information on swell, which is difficult to predict using simpler numerical models of wave generation.

— Inshore wave monitoring provides valuable data to complement and validate numerical modelling results. The deployment of a wave recorder at a particular site, typically for a minimum period of six months over a winter, should be carefully considered, for all significant coastal defence schemes, to provide validation data for wave prediction methods.

5.2.2.5 Coastal defences. The standard of defence and residual life of existing coastal structures will influence the evolution of a shoreline and consequently the damage that will occur to assets close to the coast. Full details of all existing structures must therefore be obtained, to assess both their residual life, and whether they can be restored to an acceptable condition.

The performance of existing defences should also be monitored, to identify maintenance costs and to assess functional performance, e.g. noting overtopping during storms and their effects on beach levels. They may have effects on coastal processes or the local environment; data collection may therefore be needed to quantify these effects, for example with a view to mitigation or enhancement measures. The history of earlier defences can be important in determining the longer-term shoreline evolution and also in providing data on performance, particularly if there has been a failure.

5.2.3 Data on benefits and costs

At each stage in the appraisal process, it will be necessary to evaluate at an appropriate level the cost of building various defence options. At the shoreline management plan stage it will only be possible to use broad-scale cost assessments based on a range of typical cost/metre run values for a range of defence types and standards. As the options are developed, more detailed evaluations of the costs (and benefits) can be made (see Section 6.2). If at any stage it becomes evident that the costs required for all defence options are significantly greater than the benefits delivered by those options, it would be prudent to accept that trying to defend the area is inappropriate.

The most obvious benefits of coastal defence arise from the avoidance of flooding or coastal erosion. Flooding may arise from overflow, wave overtopping or breaching of a natural or man-made sea-defence structure. If property, infrastructure or other man-made or natural assets would have been lost or damaged but for the presence of a defence then the avoidance of this loss represents an economic benefit of the defence. Therefore, it is necessary to collect data on the property that will be damaged. This will include type, age and value of residential property; area, construction type, use and contents of commercial property; details of infrastructure such as roads, railways and utilities; and the areas and classification of agricultural land that might be affected.

There may also be loss of amenities and recreation assets and the avoidance of such losses or the enhancement of existing assets at or close to the shoreline arising as a direct consequence of the proposed works may be counted as benefits arising from a scheme. If possible, data to evaluate these, such as changes in visitor numbers or income should be collected. Data will be necessary to evaluate other indirect benefits arising from prevention of disruption and avoidance of recovery costs for example. The possible risk to life should also be assessed but some human impacts, such as those on health, stress and loss of memorabilia are not easily valued in economic terms, although this is an active area of research at present. Nevertheless, any available data such as the numbers of people likely to be affected should be collected.

5.2.4 Data on environmental constraints and opportunities

Either the removal or the construction of coastal defences can have significant impacts on the environment, both natural and man-made. The need to conserve and enhance the environment will be the prime objective of coastal defences in some locations but can be a significant constraint on their design/construction elsewhere. There is therefore a need to gather information to assess the environmental effects of alternative management options.

The environmental attributes of the coastal zone are normally classified in five categories:

1. biological
2. socio-economic
3. physical
4. aesthetic
5. chemical.

Each of these categories of environmental attributes is briefly discussed further below. More detailed discussion on data collection for environmental impact assessments is provided in Section 6.3.

5.2.4.1 Biological attributes. Any scheme on the coast has the potential to cause changes to the biology of a site or area. In some cases, the biological characteristics of a coastal site may prove to be of critical or dominant importance in management decision making. Biological resources that potentially might be influenced include terrestrial, coastal and marine habitats. Other activities such as fishing or recreation that depend on these resources might also be affected.

A broad understanding is therefore required of the types of habitat, the presence of any rare species, and their potential sensitivity to change. As with the other parameters, more detailed information will also be required in some areas, notably for sites where the biological assets are protected and/or particularly vulnerable. Many environmentally important areas will have special protection from development, for example those in the UK being designated as a Site of Special Scientific Interest (SSSI), a Special Protection Area (SPA) or a Special Area of Conservation (SAC). In such cases, the designations will mean that information on the biological interests of the site will have been well documented. Details will need to be obtained of any existing plans relating to the management of such designated areas. On a more general level, protection of the biodiversity of an area is important and, if there is not already an assessment of the existing biodiversity, one will need to be made. Where it is not possible to avoid loss of existing habitat, especially if it has been designated, then information should be collected on areas where schemes to mitigate or compensate for any losses may be undertaken.

5.2.4.2 Physical attributes. The physical processes operating on a coast are fundamentally important in establishing its environmental characteristics. In some cases, habitats will depend on the existing erosion and sediment transport regime, for example the interchange of sand between dunes and beaches. Similarly, seawater clarity may be affected by adding fine-grained beach material, and geological interests may depend on continued erosion and exposure of a cliff face or on the preservation of a particular type and grading of beach sediments. These environmental concerns may be at the site where defences are being considered or some distance away, typically along the downdrift coastline. Particular care will be needed when defences are being considered near a site designated for its geological or geomorphological interest.

5.2.4.3 Socio-economic attributes. The importance of the coastline as a recreational asset must be recognized in any coastal defence initiative. Many coastal towns and cities depend for their economic wellbeing on tourism and recreation which, in turn, depends on the quality of the beach and seafront. Aspects such as ease of access to the beach for pedestrians, or the provision of launching facilities for fishing boats, recreational craft or inshore lifeboats will often be important. Some of the data needed to assess the economic consequences of changes to such attributes are covered in 5.2.3 above.

The dependence of industry or commerce on a coastal location will also need to be considered. Ports and harbours, along with some power stations and sewage treatment works require a coastal site for their effective operation. Data will have to be collected on the requirements of such operations in order that they can be accommodated in a coastal defence scheme. Similarly, there may be a need to consider impacts on infrastructure such as roads, railways, other communications and the like. Other socio-economic activities that may need to be considered include navigation, agriculture, aquaculture and wild-fowling.

5.2.4.4 Aesthetic attributes. The aesthetic characteristics of a particular stretch of coast can be extremely important in determining its use(s) and, often, its socio-economic value. Many coastlines are still unspoilt and protected by planning policies, including special designations, because of their landscape or heritage values. In contrast, the coastal defences in many resorts are important features of the seafront, and the style and landscaping of any new schemes will be carefully scrutinized by local residents, etc. Any coastal management or defence initiatives must be developed in the full understanding of these aesthetic values. Data on such designations and any particular aesthetic attributes of the area will need to be collected.

5.2.4.5 Chemical attributes. Chemical parameters that could potentially be affected by coastal defence initiatives include water and land quality. Water quality can be affected not only directly, for example by contamination with chemical substances, but also indirectly by changes in physical processes. Potential pollutants may be 'trapped' behind a breakwater, or changes in dispersion characteristics due to changes in water movements brought about by installing coastal defences. In turn, this can cause complications with respect to the operation of wastewater outfalls, etc.

5.3 Assessing the effect of not intervening

The advantages and disadvantages of any potential defence scheme always need to be compared with those of not intervening and allowing the coastline to evolve naturally. Assessing the effect of doing so will provide important information for:

— the choice and design of new defences, and
— a 'baseline' against which the economic and environmental consequences of any proposed scheme can be compared.

It should be noted that the 'no active intervention' policy of shoreline management planning (see Section 2.4) and the 'do-nothing' option of the economic appraisal (see 6.2.5 below) are not exactly the same. The latter is essentially a hypothetical test case to assess the damage that might occur in the event of not installing defences or of not rehabilitating/renewing existing ones, and must always be considered. This option assumes one will 'walk away' from a situation with the absolute minimum of action, e.g. warning notices for public safety where necessary. The policy and the option would converge when considering the need to intervene on a substantially natural coastline. This could include one where there is currently active intervention such as beach management, with or without recharge.

Where structures are involved it is likely that active intervention, by doing something such as removing the structures and allowing the shore to realign, would be the only practical strategic policy where a scheme for repairing defences or installing new ones cannot be justified. Even so, the 'do-nothing' situation will still need to be assessed as the baseline economic and environmental option. Additionally, the 'no active intervention' policy does not preclude monitoring of coastal processes and changes, which in time may indicate a different defence strategy.

Consideration of the effect of not intervening normally involves the following main steps:

— analysing and quantifying wave conditions, tides and sediment transport rates
— assessing the present condition, performance, and residual life of any existing defences
— predicting the future changes in the coastline and its beaches
— evaluating the economic and environmental consequences of such changes.

5.3.1 Assessing hydrodynamics and sediment transport rates

Whether it is eventually decided to install a defence scheme, or not to intervene, it is always useful to define, at an early stage, the waves, tides and sediment transport rates along the coastline. Normally numerical modelling and analysis will be needed to achieve these requirements. The information typically required is as follows:

— wave conditions in the area of interest, at a location just offshore from the wave breaking zone (this should include information on wave heights, periods and directions, for both regularly occurring and exceptionally severe conditions)
— tidal levels including the effects of surges, with estimates of exceptionally high levels
— information on the joint probability of large waves and high tidal levels to provide estimates of the conditions that any defence may encounter.

It may also be necessary to investigate and quantify tidal or other currents if these are strong close inshore.

From the above information, it is important to define the combinations of wave and tidal conditions that a defence scheme may experience, with a view to specifying the standards of protection against flooding or erosion that it should provide. It is also valuable to make an initial estimate of the average long-shore sediment transport rate at the site. This is an essential first step in later assessments of coastal changes and of the feasibility of beach recharge or recycling as a defence option.

Further details of all these procedures can be found in standard textbooks, such as the CIRIA *Beach Management Manual* (1996).

5.3.2 Assessing existing defences

In the UK, the choice of a new defence scheme will often be influenced by existing defences at or close to its proposed location. Assessing these existing defences is important because they will:

— influence the future evolution of the coastline and its beaches (see Section 5.1.3), and
— give guidance on the types of new defence that might be appropriate at the site.

Knowledge of the maintenance costs and past effectiveness of existing and any earlier defences, whether considered successful or not, will be useful when choosing a new scheme. Extending or adapting a successful defence for use along a nearby stretch of coast is clearly an option worth careful consideration if intervention is deemed a possibility.

Both the condition and remaining life of an existing defence need to be considered (see Figure 16). For structures that are in poor condition, the options of strengthening, extending or repair may be feasible at reasonable cost. Whether or not active intervention is being proposed, the likely timing and extent of a failure of an existing defence therefore have to be estimated. This will be an important factor in predicting how the coastline will evolve, which is essential to determine what is vulnerable and whether intervention is worthwhile. It will also be important in determining the most appropriate timing of any intervention (see Section 5.3.4 below). Furthermore, the continued presence and influence of defences, e.g. a groyne system updrift of the study area, might continue to affect the evolution of the coast where defences are being considered.

While surveying existing defences is reasonably straightforward, there is often a considerable problem in estimating how and when a structure may 'fail' and to what extent its failure will affect the adjacent coastline. A distinction also has to be made between functional and structural failures. The loss of a few planks from a wood

Figure 16   Coastal defences nearing end of useful life

groyne will greatly reduce its functional efficiency, although its structure will be largely intact. Conversely, a rock revetment may experience considerable structural damage with much of its armour displaced, but it may still largely function to prevent erosion of the cliffs behind it for a considerable time afterwards. The breaching of a seawall or embankment would result in structural and functional failure. Further reading on assessing the residual life of coastal defences can be found in a research report commissioned by DEFRA and written by Sayers and Simm (2001).

5.3.3 Predicting future changes in the coastline and standards of defence

The prediction, with reasonable accuracy, of future changes to a coastline, with and without defences, is essential if a sound decision on the need for coastal defences is to be reached. The objectives are to quantify:

— the likely landwards recession of the shoreline or cliffs and hence land losses
— the lowering of beach levels, leading to deeper water close inshore, which may increase the risk of flooding or damage
— likely changes in the standard of coastal defence, for example because of increased sea levels.

In each case, such changes may lead to increased risks to assets at or close to the shore. Changes in a coastline will inevitably depend on the wave conditions that occur and these cannot be predicted with certainty. Increasingly, therefore, predictions of coastal change are being made using statistical methods, providing a range of possible outcomes.

In such an evaluation, the logical starting place is an analysis of past shoreline changes, typically using historical maps and any beach survey data (see Section 5.2.1). Where there have not been, and are not expected to be, any significant human impacts on a coastline, and where the geology is reasonably consistent, then past changes in a coast may be a good basis for predicting future changes.

In most cases, however, account will need to be taken of the effects of coastal defences or other human interference. This will often require using a predictive model of the coastline, usually a computer simulation, or perhaps a laboratory model. As noted earlier, changes in the existing standards of defences as a consequence of not maintaining them will be an important aspect in the consideration of the both the 'no active intervention' policy of shoreline management planning and the 'do-nothing' option of economic and environmental appraisals.

5.3.4 Preliminary economic evaluation

Once the likely changes in a coastline, and any defences, have been assessed, assuming no intervention, an evaluation of the economic consequences of those changes is needed. This involves identifying assets at risk from erosion or flooding, and the benefits that can be achieved by preventing or delaying such losses. This assessment will need to identify both when and where any changes or damage will occur, so that the urgency and extent of an appropriate defence scheme can be established. A convenient basis for determining the lengths of coastline over which these appraisals are carried out are the 'management units' introduced earlier, in Section 2.3. Further details of the methods for economic and environmental evaluations are present later, in Section 6.2.

Using the economic appraisal of the effects of doing nothing, an initial view can be formed on the level of expenditure on coastal defences that may be financially justifiable along any stretch of the coastline. In many cases, this will be helpful in eliminating very expensive options that might otherwise be considered.

At a strategic level, in considering whether active intervention might be feasible, the benefits to be gained from preventing any future losses due to flooding, or erosion of assets at imminent risk, can be estimated for a stretch of coastline, e.g. a 'management unit'. The value of these benefits can then be divided by the length of coastline, and the resulting ratio then compared with outline costs of alternative shoreline management policies. Table 5.1 can be used to indicate the possible generic defence options that might be appropriate from an economic viewpoint. The more detailed economic evaluation required for the strategy and scheme design steps is covered in Section 6.2.

It must be emphasized, however, that often the most appropriate defence scheme is not the most expensive. Where an appropriate standard of protection can be provided by a simpler defence option, then this may be preferable from the viewpoints of environmental effects and sustainability.

Table 5.1

Benefit/unit length	Possible defence scheme options
<£200/m	No active or minimal intervention, e.g. monitoring, warning systems, short-term and low-cost measures to delay damage and allow orderly abandonment of assets. Minor works such as dune fencing/planting.
<£1000/m	Light defence structures, e.g. groynes or low rock revetments or sills. Beach management including recharge and recycling. Refurbishment or strengthening of existing defence structures. Cliff drainage/re-profiling.
<£5000/m	More substantial defence structures such as concrete or rock revetments, nearshore breakwaters or more extensive groyne systems together with infill beach recharge. Rebuilding/extension of existing defences.
>£5000/m	Offshore breakwaters, mass-concrete seawalls, major beach recharge schemes with groynes or recycling. Surge barriers for inlets/estuaries.

5.3.5 Preliminary environmental appraisal

At the stage of evaluating the policy of no active intervention, it is appropriate to make an initial assessment of the environmental consequences of this, or other, management policies. This can be achieved by reviewing information on the environmental attributes that might be affected (as discussed in Section 5.2.3) and by initial consultations with those with concerns or hopes for the coastal environment. The importance of the coastline as a recreational asset may be a major environmental factor in the consideration of defences in urban areas. This is less likely in more remote and rural areas, for example in estuaries, when the biological attributes of the coast often become a dominating issue.

As a general guide, adverse effects on the natural environment (e.g. geomorphology, biology) will be fewer for options such as non-intervention or beach recharge/management. In contrast, those concerned with amenity, recreation and heritage attributes may prefer options such as seawalls. However, such simple guidance will inevitably be misleading in some situations, and each stretch of coast will have to be assessed on its own environmental merits.

It is also worth noting that the introduction of a shoreline management initiative or the construction of a coastal defence scheme may be beneficial rather than harmful to some of these environmental assets and may provide opportunities for environmental enhancement. Examples are protecting a sensitive fresh-water resource against marine flooding or providing erosion protection to a tourist resort.

5.4 Public consultation

As for the preliminary appraisal of environmental effects of any defence scheme, it is important to involve the public in the process at an early stage. In most cases, coastal defences are built with the public's money for their benefit. The knowledge and perceptions of those living or working close to the coast are important both in the identification of problems and in the choice of the management strategy adopted. The objectives of any scheme will essentially comprise the requirements of people whose representatives are likely to be among those responsible for approving any schemes. It may not be possible to meet all the objectives, particularly where they are mutually incompatible, and the final scheme choice and details may well require some agreed compromises to be made.

Consultation and effective public participation in the decision making process are therefore fundamentally important in achieving an acceptable coastal defence. In addition, the public and the various bodies consulted are likely to have much of the existing physical, cost/benefit and environmental information needed to assist in making those decisions.

Such participation should involve non-statutory groups and other interested parties, such as non-governmental organizations and local residents, as well as statutory agencies such as national conservation bodies, local and national government departments, etc. To be effective, consultation needs to start early, e.g. at the initiation of any shoreline management plan, and continue throughout the decision making process. Where appropriate, this might extend up to, throughout and beyond construction into post-project monitoring and evaluation (see Sections 8.5 and 9.2).

Consultation can be either formal or informal or both. Participation might be achieved by a combination of correspondence, discussion groups, public or private meetings, exhibitions, or similar. The involvement of interested parties through this type of initiative will assist not only in the identification of issues or potential problems but also in their resolution. Discussion and negotiation, based on an understanding of all points of view (e.g. coastal defence, nature conservation, and recreation), will often facilitate the identification of a mutually acceptable way forward. This is because compromises are often required and imposing such solutions on those who have not been involved in their development can lead to conflict and delays.

5.5 Assessing coastal defence options

If at each step there is justification for proceeding with a coastal defence scheme, the next step will be to set out the possible options for more detailed assessment. It is important to consider a wide range of options, and not to dismiss any possibilities without overwhelming technical, economic or environmental reasons.

As mentioned earlier, the likelihood in the UK is that any coastal defence scheme will be influenced by existing defences either at a site of interest or adjacent to it. This leads to a range of site-specific options, depending on the condition and success of earlier schemes. These will normally be cheaper than building a completely new defence, and will often have only modest effects on the environmental character of the coastline, for example retaining much of the same appearance and amenity of the existing situation. The possible options might include:

— removal of some or all of the defence elements
— repair/refurbishment of structures to original condition
— replacement or rebuilding to original condition
— extending or strengthening existing structures to improve standard of defence
— addition of supplementary components to improve standard of defence.

For example, seawalls might be increased in height, have an apron and sheet-steel piles added to counter toe scour or be protected by the addition of a rock toe berm or a beach recharge and thus have their standard enhanced. Similarly, rock revetments or groynes might be re-built or strengthened by addition of further rock. If the failure of any part of a substantial length of defences would flood a single area, it will be necessary to consider the standards and long-term commitments for the whole frontage in a strategic manner.

For coasts where there are no existing defences, it is preferable to first consider options that are 'flexible', rather than 'fixing' the coastline at an early stage. For situations where beaches only experience a modest drift rate, then a beach recharge scheme is the option least likely to cause adverse environmental effects, either locally or along adjacent stretches of coast. This approach will only rarely be a permanent solution to erosion or flooding problems, but this may be an advantage, for example providing short-term protection until more information on coastal processes and evolution becomes available.

Where beach recharge alone is not feasible, then the addition of beach 'control' structures such as groynes or breakwaters should be considered.

Direct protection to the hinterland might be provided by the construction of structures such as clay embankments or rock revetments, depending on the intensity of the wave climate. These should be assessed, perhaps with improvements to beaches, before more expensive, permanent structures are considered.

Whatever method of coastal defence is considered, so too must the sequence and timing of any works. In some cases, some works may be profitably delayed because of the effect on coastal processes that works on one length may have on another. This may affect the timing of later defence works, or even the type of works that are chosen.

Finally, where defences are required for a substantial interrelated length of shoreline, or where works will need to be phased over several years, then a strategy for their implementation will be necessary.

6. Choosing a preferred option

Selecting the best scheme for managing or defending a coast is often a difficult task. As it should be clear from Chapter 5, it is important *not* to choose a single option at too early a stage. Much effort in detailed design may be wasted if unforeseen difficulties arise later, e.g. a major environmental objection, or increases in the cost of materials. Similarly, new opportunities may arise; for example, availability of dredged material suitable for beach recharge, influencing the selection process. The selection of a preferred option is best achieved by eliminating options until a shortlist of the feasible ones is achieved. These may not all be different technical solutions, but variations on the same solution with a range of design standards, giving different costs and benefits. For example, a range of seawall crest heights could be investigated. The appraisal techniques described in this chapter do not apply just to the final choice of the preferred option. They should be used throughout the choosing of options, from shoreline management plan through the strategy plan stage, at increasing levels of rigour, eliminating some in the process. A preferred option is likely to be subjected to the most rigorous appraisal.

The purpose of appraisal is to assess the suitability of various coastal defence options in terms of technical, environmental and economic criteria. It is also necessary, at this stage, to assess the various risks associated with each option in detail. The appraisal process leads to the selection of a preferred option or scheme. It may be that the preferred option is clearly evident but, where this is not the case, further more detailed studies will be required to select the preferred one (e.g. physical model studies, ecological monitoring, contingent valuation survey/analysis).

Sometimes, a type of defence can immediately be ruled out on technical grounds. In many other cases, however, economic or environmental considerations lead to possible options being excluded from further detailed consideration. In some cases, it may be that differences in risk, perhaps of risk of failure, of damage to the environment or cost certainty may sway the final choice.

These four aspects of appraisal are now described in turn, although it must be emphasized that they must be viewed together. A perfect solution is virtually impossible and the preferred option must be a balance between acceptability on all four counts.

6.1 Technical appraisal

6.1.1 Introduction

The technical appraisal of existing or proposed coastal defence schemes has to address four main issues:

— functional effectiveness; will it work? Does it meet the objectives set for it?
— durability and residual life; will the scheme continue to perform its intended purpose for the projected scheme life?
— sustainability; will it prejudice the attainment of objectives in the future?
— 'constructability'; can the scheme be built safely, and at reasonable cost, at the particular site of interest?

To successfully undertake the technical appraisal, some aspects of preliminary design for each of the options may need to be undertaken, as described in Chapter 7. Each of the above four points is discussed further in the following sections (6.1.2−6.1.3).

6.1.2 Functional effectiveness

The functional effectiveness of a coastal defence is measured primarily by its ability to reduce flooding (sea defence) and/or erosion (coast protection). The appraisal will consider whether an option adequately reduces the probability of failure of a defence. This should include estimating both the chances of structural failure, and of functional failure, i.e. of severe conditions causing overtopping or damage. The performance of a defence depends upon its 'hydraulic profile' (e.g. the seawall height, slope and roughness; or beach volume, slope and porosity) and on its plan shape (e.g. its alignment to the incident wave crests and to the shoreline). The technical appraisal has to determine the effectiveness of the scheme for various sets of design conditions of waves and water levels. It is unlikely that a solution that will totally protect against flooding or stand up to any storm on the open coastline will be economic. There must be a balance between the cost of a scheme and the benefits gained in reduction of damage (see Section 6.2, Economic appraisal).

It is also important to realize that the assessment of functional effectiveness should include an appraisal of changes in the conditions at the defence and the design parameters. There may be changes in the environment, for example an increase in mean sea level or a change in the wave climate. Often, however, it is a lowering of the level of the beach, or the shore platform, just in front of the defences that is most important. An increased water depth at the toe of the defence will allow larger waves to reach it, and may lead to scour and subsequent damage to the structure. An estimation of how beach levels could change during its lifetime, and subsequent calculations of the effectiveness of the defence under these conditions, is therefore an essential part of the design process.

The effectiveness of a coastal defence scheme is sometimes expressed in terms of the 'standard of defence' it provides. The standard of defence is defined by the probability of exceedence of an extreme water level, extreme wave condition, or combination of both, during which the defence would fail to provide effective protection. An advantage of this approach is that the required level of protection can be related to design water levels, or wave conditions, whose individual or joint probability can be specified in advance of the design of a coastal defence structure.

The concept of 'standard of defence' can be readily applied to flood protection, in which the standard refers to the probability of an event that would result in inundation, either by overtopping or by a breach. The same idea is sometimes applied to coastal protection works, although with greater difficulty. Such a standard can, for example, be evaluated in terms of the probability of an event that would cause rapid erosion of a beach thus exposing hard defences behind, or that would cause failure of a structure or a major cliff-top recession. However, the evaluation of this type of response is generally more difficult than predicting whether given combinations of water level and waves will overtop a flood embankment.

There are various ways of expressing the probability of an event. Although the return period, e.g. one in 100 years, has often been used, this terminology can cause confusion to those who think that if an event of one in 100-year return period has just occurred, it will not occur again for another 100 years. Current research is examining ways in which such risks can be most appropriately communicated. In advance of these findings, it is preferable to express an event in terms of its annual probability of occurrence, for example a 1% chance (or probability of 0.01) of occurring (or being exceeded) in any year.

It may also be helpful to calculate the likelihood of an event exceeding a particular standard of defence in the lifetime of the structure. For example, there is a 39% chance that an event with a one in 100-year return period, or a more severe one, will occur during a scheme service life of 50 years. As will be seen later, such information is crucial to the assessment of damages that can still occur with a new or replacement defence in place.

6.1.3 Durability and residual life

New coastal defences are planned with an operational or service life typically of about 50 years, and the technical assessment has to address the durability of the scheme and its components over that time. When assessing existing defences, the same principles apply but the objective is to determine the residual life, i.e. the remaining part of the useful (service) life of the structure (see Figure 17). The concepts of service or design working life, and of residual life, are very important in the economic assessment of coastal defence. They determine the benefits of early intervention and thus form the basis for determining appropriate future expenditure on maintenance and/or capital works.

Damage rates to structures such as seawalls and beach control structures (settlement, abrasion, armour instability, geotechnical instability, etc.), and to soft defences such as beaches or saltmarshes (profile erosion, long-shore realignment, degradation of saltmarsh surface, etc.) have to be estimated. Alternative techniques and materials have to be considered as part of the technical appraisal process; indeed it is usually required to demonstrate to the funding agencies that variants have been properly considered in the whole appraisal process. These may result from structural changes, for example as a rock revetment suffers cumulative damage over a number of years.

The durability of a given defence also depends on the maintenance programme that should form part of the overall defence scheme. In the case of a beach recharge scheme, 'maintenance' by way of future recharge operations (to make good sediment losses) is usually a pre-requisite and essential component of the project. The choice of options may need to be made between schemes that have high and low maintenance requirements. In addition to the relative economic differences, consideration needs to be given to the likelihood of maintenance being undertaken in an adequate and timely fashion to maintain the required standard of service.

Figure 17   Assets at risk from cliff recession

6.1.4 Sustainability

A commonly accepted definition of sustainability is that of Bruntland (World Commission on Environment and Development, 1987) namely:

development that meets the needs of the present without compromising the ability of future generations to meet their own needs

Sustainable coastal defence schemes have been defined (Ministry of Agriculture, Fisheries and Food/Welsh Office, 1993) as:

... schemes which take account of the interrelationships with other defences, developments and processes within a coastal cell, and which avoid as far as possible tying future generations into inflexible and expensive options for coastal defence.

Consider, for example, an eroding coastline with a sea wall that protects low-lying land from flooding. If the beach in front of the wall is progressively lowering, and the wall itself needs raising to cope with increasing sea levels and overtopping, then this type of defence will not be sustainable indefinitely. However, abandoning the wall and allowing, for example, a community it protected to be destroyed would also be unsustainable.

If, however, one was to gradually relocate the assets at risk, while maintaining the seawall remained tolerable (from economic and environmental viewpoints), then a reasonably sustainable solution might be achieved.

The sustainability of a scheme is not necessarily confined to the interaction between the scheme and the environment at the site of the actual defence. It applies to influences that are remote from it. The technical appraisal has to determine whether the proposed scheme will be sustainable in the long term. In other words, will the construction or operation of the proposed scheme serve to defer, displace or even exacerbate the long-term problem? Some of the matters that have to be considered, therefore, are:

— effects of the defences on adjacent shorelines, and on the adjacent seabed and hinterland
— effects of long-term trends (changes in design storm conditions, coastal recession, etc.), and
— long-term availability of resources (e.g. recharge material for shingle beaches).

6.1.5 Constructability

Finally, the technical appraisal has to address the constructability of the coastal defence. This issue is also discussed in BS6349, Part 1. Amongst the items that need to be considered are:

— availability of materials, e.g. it is often more economic to use concrete armour in place of rock, for rock sizes greater than about 20 tonnes (although this choice may involve 'sustainability' issues)
— access to the site for plant and materials; consider whether materials are to be delivered by road (route, width and conditions of roads?) or by sea (depth of water close to site to unload materials?) — see also Section 8.1
— inter-tidal working — whether working by land-based or floating plant, limitations in the 'tidal window' can significantly affect the construction time and hence the programme to meet target deadlines — see Section 8.2
— risks due to weather e.g. arrangements for the works be secured in the event of an impending storm — see Section 8.3
— geotechnical suitability of the site for the proposed structure
— tolerances of work — especially working below water (e.g. dredging, recharge, and the construction of revetment toe).

The need to bear all of these factors in mind from the earliest stage in choosing possible coastal defence schemes is crucially important, to avoid undue risk and expense during construction and in subsequent maintenance operations.

6.2 Economic appraisal

Economic appraisal is a technique to determine whether investment in coastal defence works is worthwhile in comparison with other publicly funded projects. It also provides a method to determine the appropriate standard of the defence.

6.2.1 Introduction

In principle, there is no difference between the economic appraisal of coastal defence and other civil engineering projects. However, the difficulty of evaluating the potential effects of natural events that occur in an unpredictable manner offers challenges that are specific to this type of work. In the UK, the Treasury provides guidance on methods of appraising public projects. Specific guidance (Flood and Coastal Defence, Project Appraisal Guidance Notes) interpreting these requirements for flood and coastal defence projects in England and Wales has been produced by Ministry of Agriculture, Fisheries and Food (now DEFRA). This series of documents should be considered as a whole, but Volume 3 (FCDPAG3) deals specifically with economic appraisal.

6.2.2 Present values/ discounting

Discounting is a standard technique used to obtain the present value of both costs incurred and benefits generated throughout the appraisal period. This provides a common basis for analysing alternative solutions that offer very different standards of protection or those that involve different timing of investment. For example, it may be necessary to compare a high-standard, high-cost scheme with one that offers a lower standard of protection at significantly lower cost. The same approach can also be applied to compare, for example, a beach management solution involving high recurrent expenditure for recycling with one involving a large capital investment in beach control structures.

The time-span considered in an appraisal will usually extend to the end of the operational or service life of any major capital works (the time when they would be expected to need complete reconstruction or major rehabilitation). Where continuing expenditure is planned, an appraisal period of at least 50 years ensures that, through discounting, changes outside the appraisal period are unlikely to have a significant economic impact on the final decision. In the UK, the discount rate for investment in public works is set by the Treasury, and similar arrangements may be in place elsewhere. Where there is no set rate it may be necessary to assess what effect changes in the discount rate would have on the economic appraisal of options.

6.2.3 Costs

The costs of alternative engineering or management options should include capital works as well as all ongoing maintenance expenditure required to provide the determined standard of service for the whole of the appraisal period. Often the timing and extent of this expenditure cannot be estimated accurately; so it may be necessary to undertake a probabilistic assessment. If, for example, a beach recharge is likely to be required within a particular five-year period, it may be appropriate to develop a probability profile for this activity and multiply the costs by the appropriate probability factors to determine an expected value. All costs over the appraisal period have to be discounted to a common time-base, i.e. at the start of the appraisal period, to determine the total present value cost of the scheme.

6.2.4 Benefits

Because coastal storms that cause flooding and erosion incidents are chance events whose time of occurrence is not predictable, an expected annual damage must be derived for economic evaluation purposes. This is derived as the integration of all possible damage events, multiplied by their respective probabilities, to give the expected damage in any one year. In practice, a damage/probability graph is constructed using discrete events and the expected annual damage is calculated as the area under the curve. Annual probabilities may change over time. For example, if a seawall is deteriorating, or a beach is reducing in width, then the probability of a breach will increase year by year. Alternatively the probability of different water levels may change over time due to combined land-level movements and sea-level rise. The present value of damage for any scenario is the sum of expected annual damages discounted over the project life to the appraisal date. A similar probabilistic approach should be adopted for the timing of potential erosion events.

In the UK, standard tables are available to evaluate damage to property for different building classifications and depths and durations of flooding (see Parker et al., 1987 and Penning-Rowsell et al., 1992). These publications also give methods for calculating other tangible economic losses. These may include disruption to roads or railways, damage to public amenities and reduction or loss of recreational opportunities.

Intangible elements of damage, such as changes to natural habitats, may not be so readily amenable to evaluation. Some techniques such as contingent valuation methodology (CVM) may be applied but require specialist advice and input (see Ministry of Agriculture, Fisheries and Food, 1999).

Where damage can be caused by a combination of different factors, such as waves and high tidal levels, then a joint probability analysis must be carried out. It is important for the economic and performance analysis of the defence that the probabilities assigned are a true representation of the damage probabilities from whatever combination of events (see Owen et al., 1997).

In assessing benefits for all publicly funded projects, it will usually be necessary to ensure that all benefits and 'disbenefits' are taken into account and that the benefits are expressed in economic rather than financial terms. For example, improvement in a beach at one resort may attract tourists from a nearby one with little real economic gain and arguably a net overall loss. Such 'disbenefits' should also be included in any assessment.

6.2.5 Economic comparison of options

The starting point for any economic appraisal is consideration of the 'do-nothing' option in which existing defences are abandoned and no further works of construction or maintenance are undertaken (see Section 5.3). The resulting damages provide a baseline against which other options can be evaluated and to give a measure of absolute economic return. A sufficient range of other scenarios should then be considered to derive an optimum solution. In the case of publicly financed defences, where there is a scarcity of overall funding, this is usually defined as the solution with the highest 'benefit/cost ratio', provided that this exceeds unity. The benefit/cost ratio is the total present value of benefits of the scheme divided by total present value of the costs of the scheme.

However, this general preference for a scheme with the highest benefit/cost ratio should be considered in relation the standard of defence provided (see FCDPAG 3). In general, the 'marginal benefit/cost ratio' of a higher-standard option (the additional benefit derived from providing the higher standard divided by the extra cost of providing that standard) should be considered in relation to the benefits that could be gained by investing the extra money elsewhere.

As with all aspects of project appraisal, the results and assumptions should be subjected to appropriate sensitivity testing to determine whether the resultant decision is robust. It is also important to look at other decision techniques where, for example, there are major differences between options in terms of impact on environmental or other assets that are not amenable to accurate economic evaluation.

6.3 Environmental appraisal

6.3.1 Background and need for environmental appraisal

An environmental appraisal for a coastal management or defence initiative can be undertaken at different levels of detail depending on the procedures being followed and the sensitivity of the affected site. In support of the final choice, and in the case of some strategy plans, a formal environmental impact assessment leading to the production of an environmental statement may be required. The relevant legislation governing environmental impact assessments for coastal defence works in the UK is given in the box below.

> For schemes where Planning Approval is required, *The Town and Country Planning (Environmental Impact Assessment) (England and Wales) Regulations 1999 – SI 1999 No. 293* will apply. This will include all coast protection works and new sea defence works.
>
> For sea/flood defence improvement works, for which there is deemed planning consent, *The Environmental Impact Assessment (Land Drainage Improvement Works) Regulations 1999 – SI 1999 No. 1783* will apply.

At a less formal level, an environmental appraisal will be required. This follows the same general procedures as a formal environmental impact assessment, but the coverage might be more targeted or less rigorous, or for example, alternative options might not be covered in detail. Further details on wider aspects of environmental appraisal, including dealing with designated sites of international importance, and on valuation, are covered in the Ministry of Agriculture, Fisheries and Food (now DEFRA) publication: Flood and Coastal Defence, Project Appraisal Guidance Notes, FCDPAG5 – Environmental Appraisal.

A formal environmental impact assessment will usually be required by the permitting or licensing agency (either directly or following a request from another statutory body) if the proposed development has the potential to significantly affect one or more environmental characteristics (see Section 5.2.3). This is most likely to be the case where the environmental parameter(s) concerned are particularly sensitive. This may be on an undeveloped coastline and/or in areas designated as being of special importance (e.g. a nationally or internationally rare species of flora or fauna). In this case, detailed investigation will generally be required. Conversely, an environmental appraisal might be carried out as a check to confirm that there are no significant impacts, to resolve a particular problem, or simply as a matter of good practice.

Finally, it should be noted that the purpose of either an environmental appraisal or impact assessment is to identify the option with the least adverse environmental impact. It is not supposed to be used as a damage limitation exercise. Wherever possible, the technique should therefore be applied early, at a stage where a range of options is being assessed. It should not be used simply to reduce impacts and hence try to make a pre-selected option more environmentally acceptable. Wherever possible, environmental enhancement should be sought in conjunction with keeping environmental impacts to a minimum (see Section 6.3.5).

6.3.2 Scoping

Scoping is potentially the most important step in the environmental appraisal process. Scoping is the mechanism by which potential issues related to any of the environmental parameters discussed in Section 5.2 are identified. An initial appraisal is then undertaken in order to ensure that potentially significant impacts are identified. Properly carried out, scoping should help to ensure that the correct level of consideration is given to those impacts that require careful investigation and that resources are targeted accordingly. It should help to establish whether or not a particular resource is particularly sensitive and whether there is sufficient existing information to ensure a satisfactory evaluation of the potential impact(s). Used effectively, scoping can therefore help to facilitate the production of a robust report, which deals directly with the issues of consequence, but at minimum cost to the promoter of a coastal defence scheme.

Scoping can be carried out in a number of ways. Site visits and a literature search will usually be important initial steps. Experiences from previous or similar initiatives should be identified and drawn upon. Consultation with interested parties, both statutory and non-statutory (see Section 5.4), will also be useful, not only in identifying issues of concern (and hence potential objections should these issues remain unresolved), but also in highlighting any existing data held by that organization or others. Using existing data can be especially cost-effective in environmental appraisal both because it reduces the cost of original survey work and because it provides a 'historical perspective' which cannot otherwise be obtained without potentially significant delays to the proposed scheme.

6.3.3 Environmental surveys

The scoping exercise will have identified (some of) the data requirements for the environmental appraisal and given some indication of the priority of obtaining data on different parameters. The data collection undertaken in the preliminary stages should identify any existing data that may be useful, such as any that might be held by statutory agencies (in the UK for example, the Environment Agency, Ministry of Agriculture, Fisheries and Food, English Nature, Countryside Council for Wales, etc.). Universities, NGOs, voluntary groups, and others may have collected other data. Existing information, provided it is reliable (data collected by students, for example, should not generally be relied upon unless it can be demonstrated that controls on its collection were very tight), can provide an invaluable input to the Environmental Appraisal process as indicated above. Existing or historic trends or changes can be identified, time and money can sometimes be saved if new data do not need to be collected, and a more robust analysis is possible.

Where necessary data do not exist and new data are to be collected, surveys must be carefully designed and monitored. This is important, not only to ensure that the results are both useful and credible, but also to provide a baseline against which subsequent monitoring results can be compared. New data, which might typically be required for a coastal defence scheme, could include information on coastal flora and fauna, water or sediment quality, traffic, noise, or archaeology. However, information requirements can vary significantly from site to site, and it is not therefore possible to provide a definitive list.

Data can be collected at various levels of detail, spatial or temporal coverage, and so on. Where appropriate, guidance on the data to be collected might be sought from the responsible (statutory) agency. This will not only help to ensure that the responsible body is 'on board', but also that the data collected is necessary and sufficient.

6.3.4 Impact identification and evaluation

Consultation and the involvement of interested parties play an important role in impact identification. So too does scientific analysis and experience. The scoping exercise will often have identified many of the potentially significant impacts, but the use of matrices and/or checklists at subsequent stages throughout the environmental appraisal is still recommended.

Once identified, an appropriate level of analysis will be required in order to establish or predict the potential significance of each potential impact. Where there is a potentially significant impact related to coastal process changes (e.g. increased wave energy leading to increased rates of erosion), it may be possible to draw on the computer modelling or physical modelling carried out as part of the design process to assist with the impact evaluation (see Chapter 7). Potential water quality impacts might similarly be subject to modelling. The evaluation of other impacts, however, might be more subjective and a judgement might have to be taken, in association with the relevant statutory authorities if appropriate, as to the significance and/or the acceptability of a particular impact.

Under the terms of the EC Directive that introduced Environmental Impact Assessment requirements to the UK, a great deal of emphasis is placed on the expected significance of an impact. Determining the significance of an impact might be achieved through a process of comparing measured and/or predicted figures to standards or norms. It may involve reference to previous research studies or the results of monitoring. However, this is often very difficult, and would normally be considered in conjunction with expertise provided by one of the statutory conservation or countryside agencies. Impacts arising from the construction stage of a proposed development may need to be evaluated separately from those associated with its final state and operation.

6.3.5 Mitigation, compensation and enhancement

Where a potential adverse impact is identified, options for mitigation should usually be considered. This becomes particularly important if the expected impact is defined as moderate or major. Environmental appraisals will indicate the expected significance of an impact both before the implementation of any mitigation measures, and after these measures are taken. The impact assuming the mitigation measures are effectively implemented is referred to as the residual impact. Where potential adverse residual impacts remain after mitigation, this could potentially threaten the viability of the proposed development.

In addition to mitigation measures (the implementation of which might be required, inter alia, by the conditions of a planning permission), enhancement measures might also be investigated and recommended. The objective of mitigation is to ensure that the present 'condition' of a particular attribute either *in situ* or elsewhere does not deteriorate to an unacceptable extent. 'Enhancement' generally refers to an initiative that is intended to result in an improvement to the existing situation.

In some cases, it may not be possible to mitigate against environmental damage by preventing deterioration to an unacceptable extent, but the opportunity exists for a different but equally valuable attribute to be created. For example, if an ecologically valuable, muddy foreshore is being eroded, threatening a flood embankment, it may not be possible to maintain that foreshore. However, by setting back the defence line it may be possible to create an additional inter-tidal area in compensation for the loss of the mudflats.

6.4 Risk

Risk is a combination of the likelihood and the consequences of an event. It must be considered throughout the design and construction of coastal defences. In this section, the risks associated with scheme performance and cost that might affect its choice and design are discussed. Risks associated more specifically with health and safety issues during construction and use are discussed in Chapter 7.

Using a risk based approach is particularly important in coastal defence because of the uncertainties associated with the events being considered and the major effects these can have on performance and life of structures, and on costs and benefits. As will have been realized from some of the previous sections of this chapter, a risk-based approach is integral to the technical and economic appraisal of options. The probability of severe events and the structural damage they are likely to cause to a defence are a primary consideration in the technical appraisal. Estimating the damage avoided by protection against events of various probabilities is usually essential for assessing benefits of a scheme. There may also be significant risks of cost increases associated with certain scheme options. Assessments should ideally also include sensitivity testing of the proposed defence scheme, by estimating how effective it will be assuming modest variations in the selected design parameters. The risks of damage to the environment should also be assessed.

These are fairly straightforward examples. Recognizing the complete range of risks that needs to be considered is more complex, but need not be difficult. There are various techniques available to help and, in any event, initial appraisal should be at a broad-brush level to identify the more important risks. One such technique is the use of either fault trees or event trees. These begin either with various modes of failure and develop the various reasons for the failure, or with the event, and develop through a tree the possible failure modes related to the event (see for examples CIRIA/CUR, 1991). Probabilities can be assigned to each consequence and risks assessed.

Risk registers are a useful aid to hazard identification, which then allows recording of the information about the risk and documentation of the decisions taken. While in some cases it may be possible to avoid risks, it is more likely that they will somehow have to be reduced, managed or mitigated. For example, it might be more cost effective to adopt a safer option at a higher initial cost, than to risk problems during either construction or the life of a scheme. The main purpose of the risk assessment at the appraisal stage is to judge how robust each option is to the possible risks that could affect it. This assessment should also consider how those risks might be managed or reduced by the selection of an appropriate option. Good risk management leads to better decision making and thus better use of resources.

Further details about the use of risk in project appraisal are contained in the Ministry of Agriculture, Fisheries and Food/DEFRA publication FCDPAG4 – *Flood and Coastal Defence Project Appraisal Guidance: Approaches to Risk* (2000).

7. Design development

7.1 Introduction

This chapter describes the final design stage for the preferred coastal defence option. Both an outline design and the desired defence standards will have been selected; these now need to be refined to produce the design of the scheme that is to be installed. This detailed design stage will be similar to the final design process for other civil engineering projects in many respects, and these will not be covered here. However, there are some unusual and important differences in the design of coastal defences that do need to be highlighted, and this is the principal aim of this chapter.

The various techniques described in this chapter may also be needed at an earlier stage, i.e. during the selection of options, in order to determine whether a scheme is feasible. For example, some detailed consideration may have been needed to calculate the dimensions of a structure so the costs can be quantified for benefit/cost analyses. Similarly, when beach recharge schemes are being contemplated, the initial volume of sediment needed, and losses over the scheme life, may be critical to both technical and economic appraisal. Evaluating these aspects will typically involve computational modelling. For other types of defence schemes, less in the way of detailed design may have been necessary to determine its technical and economic feasibility.

Note that even at the final design stage for a preferred option, the rigorous appraisal process may reveal technical or environmental problems, or unexpected costs or risks, not previously appreciated. Because of this, a revised review of the other options may be required. In the quest for the best solution, such a review should not be avoided. The final design stage will typically comprise the following components:

— refinement of structural design
— choice of materials
— safety and construction issues
— revision of environmental appraisal/assessment
— aesthetic/landscaping aspects.

7.1.1 Refinement of structural design

This will primarily involve developing such matters as the final profiles of structures, sizes of armour, heights of embankments and other details. To produce the optimum solution, numerical or physical modelling are often used, singly or in combination (see Sections 7.2 and 7.3).

In many cases, the detailed design can require striking a balance between different factors. For example, where a rock structure has been chosen there will be a balance between the slope of any seaward face and the size of the rock armour. This may be determined by the size of rock available, and the practicalities of transporting and placing it. It would be expected that some consideration of approximate slopes and armour sizes would have been undertaken, probably using one of the standard formulae (e.g. Hudson, Van der Meer) to enable cost to be estimated at option appraisal stage. At the final design stage, these will need to be refined. The refinement might be undertaken by modelling, for example of structures with an unusual cross-sectional shape, e.g. with a berm, or where limiting overtopping was critical. Similarly, it may be necessary to refine the profile shape or crest level of a sea wall to optimize its performance with regard to overtopping rates or preventing scour at its toe.

Detailed information on coastal defence design can be found in the publications listed in Box 7.1.

7.1.2 Choice of materials

The choice of materials used in a coastal defence may well be a matter for final design. For example, choices may have to be made between rock and concrete armour units for breakwaters, reinforced or mass-concrete for seawalls, sand or shingle for beach recharge schemes. Much will depend on available sources and costs at the time as well as suitability. There may be a choice of materials for use in a revetment (see 4.2.3) depending, in part on such matters as aesthetics. Such decisions may only be finalized at a late stage, in consultation with the appropriate planning authority.

Box 7.1 Publications on the design of coastal defences

The following publications provide details on various aspects of the design of coastal defence structures:

— *Seawall Design* (Thomas and Hall, 1992)
— *Beach Management Manual* (CIRIA, 1996)
— *Manual on the Use of Rock in Coastal and Shoreline Engineering* (CUR/CIRIA, 1991)
— *Revetment Systems Against Wave Attack – A Design Manual* (McConnell, 1998)
— *Manual on Artificial Beach Nourishment* (Delft Hydraulics Laboratory, 1987)
— *Guide to the use of Groynes in Coastal Engineering* (Fleming, 1990)
— *Coastal Dune Management Guide* (Ranwell and Boar, 1986)
— *A Guide to Managing Coastal Erosion in Beach Dune Systems* (Scottish Natural Heritage, 2000)
— *Overtopping of Seawalls – Design and Assessment Manual* (Environment Agency, 1999)
— *Concrete in Coastal Structures* (ed. R. T. Allen, 1998).

Relevant BSI codes, especially:
— BS6349-1: *Maritime Structures – General criteria*
— BS6349-7: *Maritime Structures – Guide to the design and construction of breakwaters.*

In addition, the United States Army Corps of Engineers (USACE) has also published the following manuals, which may be of interest to those designing

---

coastal defence structures. These are available on the Internet at: http://www.usace.army.mil/inet/usace-docs/eng-manuals:

— *Design of Coastal Revetments, Seawalls and Bulkheads*, EM 1110-2-1614
— *Coastal Groins and Nearshore Breakwaters*, EM 1110-2-1617
— *Design of Breakwaters and Jetties*, EM 1110-2-2904.

The marine environment is very aggressive and any iron or steel components need special attention. Extra cover needs to be given to reinforcement and a high cement content used to lessen the risk of water penetration within concrete, even where there is apparently little risk of abrasion. On beaches with pebbles or gravel, abrasion problems can be very severe, leading to structural damage and danger to beach users (see Figures 18 and 19). To reduce such damage, aggregate harder than the beach sediments, and high quality cement, should be used. Failing to attend to these details could lead to premature failure of a structure, or at the least, expensive repairs.

7.1.3 Safety and construction issues

Designs may need to take account of the need for tidal working during construction (see Section 8.1), or for the possibility of sudden storms. They should ensure that the defences are not vulnerable to breaching or overtopping during construction or at risk of serious damage or destruction when only partly complete. Similarly, access to sites

Figure 18   Stone steps abraded by beach shingle

Figure 19 Abrasion of face of concrete seawall

where defences are to be installed can be problematical and thus affect the type of structure that can be safely built (see Section 8.1 for further discussion of this issue).

As with all construction schemes, a risk analysis should have been undertaken at the option appraisal stage and a risk register may have been prepared. This should be revisited at the design stage as well as consideration being given to risks during construction and operation that can be eliminated or mitigated by appropriate design. In the UK, these requirements are governed by Health and Safety Legislation and the Construction Design and Management (CDM) Regulations. Further discussion of these regulations is presented in Section 8.7 of this guide.

7.1.4 Revision of environmental appraisal/impact assessment

Detailed design will also need to consider other environmental aspects of the design, some of which may have been covered by the environmental appraisal or impact assessment (see Section 6.3). These might include the need to protect certain habitats or species near the works, the need to provide access to beaches and facilities for those using the foreshore such as fishermen. Tourism is often crucial to seaside towns and the design of structures must be appropriate for the use of visitors. This might involve putting a wave wall to the rear of a promenade rather than at the fronting seawall, and ensuring the promenade is adequate to withstand the wave action on it. Where a source of material has not been covered by an environmental impact assessment, one may be necessary at this stage. It may be that only an outline environmental appraisal has been undertaken when the choice of option was made, in which case a full environmental impact assessment may be needed at the design stage to meet with statutory requirements.

7.1.5 Aesthetic/ landscaping aspects

Matters such as the aesthetics of the scheme and any landscaping and accommodation works need to be considered in the final design, although the effect on the landscape as a whole should have been considered by the environmental appraisal (see Figure 20). Coastal defences should, as far as practicable, always be in keeping with the character of the coastline. This is particularly important in seaside resorts, where surface finishes, provision of pedestrian and vehicle access, safety rails, lighting and the like may provoke major public interest and therefore affect the granting of planning permission (see Section 7.4).

7.2 Mathematical modelling

Mathematical models are useful tools for gaining an appreciation of relevant coastal processes and also for determining the impact of works on the near-shore regime and assisting in the design of coastal defence schemes. They can stand-alone or be used in tandem with physical models, depending on the problem that is being investigated. It should always be remembered, however, that the coastal zone is complex and changeable. Results from models that have not been validated for the specific location may be subject to considerable uncertainty, and the effects of potential inaccuracies

Figure 20 Landscaping behind coastal defences

should always be considered in a design process. Mathematical modelling should be regarded as an aid to understanding and quantifying natural processes, supporting not replacing observations, measurements, engineering experience and judgement.

The types of problems that can be tackled with mathematical models are as follows.

7.2.1 Predicting wave conditions

Given a coherent time series of wind velocities, then wave hindcasting models are effective in defining the equivalent time series of wave height, period and direction. This is achieved by the application of parametric equations that have been developed for both deep and shallow water from measured data. More sophisticated models which use complex wind fields to derive spatially varying wave fields are used, for example by the Meteorological Office, to carry out wave forecasting around the British Isles. The archived predictions are a very useful source of long-term data.

7.2.2 Wave transformation

As waves approach the shore, they change height and direction in response to the near-shore bathymetry. Wave refraction models are capable of predicting the consequential redistribution of energy that occurs. If seabed changes are rapid or there are surface piercing structures, wave diffraction processes can also be included. Some models can predict the effects of wave/current interactions and/or wave reflections from steeply sloping or vertically faced structures.

7.2.3 Tidal flows

Tidal and fluvial flows can be well represented in two-dimensional depth-integrated form so that dispersion processes associated with thermal cooling, water quality and sediment transport can be simulated. The last of these may also incorporate wave fields derived from wave transformation models. In estuaries, however, three-dimensional models may be needed to reproduce density current effects, particularly if pollutant dispersion is a factor in the problems being studied.

7.2.4 Beach and coastline response

Mathematical modelling of beaches can be applied at a number of different levels from one to three dimensions as follows.

— Beach profile models are used to simulate the short-term response of cross-shore beach profiles to a single wave event or a series of events, typically storm or swell conditions. These may have durations of several hours or several days and be defined in terms of wave heights, wave periods and water levels. Empirical beach profile models have been developed by curve fitting to field data or data derived from physical models. They apply to either sand beach and dune systems or shingle beaches. Process based cross-shore beach profile models include descriptions of sediment transport processes driven by non-linear wave transformations and corresponding wave driven currents in the onshore-offshore direction. Such models have only been developed for sand beaches. Beach profile models are reasonably accurate for the prediction of erosion during storms but less successful at predicting accretion during calmer wave conditions, particularly swell.
— Beach plan shape models are used to simulate the movement of a single beach contour line (so-called 'one-line models'), or of several such lines ('N-line models'), over a period ranging from several months to decades. At the simplest level, empirical curve fitting models have been derived to describe the 'equilibrium' beach plan-shape, for example between headlands or similar beach control structures, in response to waves from a 'typical' direction.

cost/high maintenance cost scheme, although low maintenance schemes at a higher capital cost may be attractive in other circumstances (see Section 6.2 above).

However, the more usual method is for a separate contract to be arranged for construction, either individually for each scheme or as a longer term partnering arrangement extending over a number of schemes. Partnering arrangements can also be made with consultants for studies into and the design of schemes.

Box 7.2 Consultation in the UK on coastal defence schemes

In England and Wales the following consultations must be undertaken.

Statutory

Consent from the DLTR under Section 34 of the Coast Protection Act 1949 for the prevention of hazard to navigation.

Licence from DEFRA under the Food and Environmental Protection Act 1985 for the prevention of pollution.

For coast protection works and new sea defences, planning approval from the local planning authority. This may also require the submission of an environmental statement.

For improvement works to existing sea defences (which do not normally require planning approval), an environmental impact assessment may be required under Environmental Impact Assessment (Land Drainage Improvement Works) Regulations 1999 – SI 1999 No. 1783.

For coast protection works, a notice in a prescribed form must be served on neighbouring authorities. County Councils (where they exist), the Environment Agency, local fisheries committees and any harbour authorities, conservancy authorities and navigation authorities.

The notice must also be published in one or more local newspapers in accordance with the appropriate regional Coast Protection Notices Regulations. *[Regulations being amended]*

Non-statutory

English Nature/Countryside Council for Wales/Scottish Natural Heritage

Ministry of Defence

The Countryside Commission (England only)

A contract will normally consist of three elements, the conditions of contract, the specification and details of the work to be carried out. There are various standard forms of these available world-wide, and which one is used will depend to a great extent on which is most suited to the situation, in particular which is in common use locally and therefore best understood.

In the UK, those forms of documentation in most common use for coastal works are:

— New Engineering Contract
— ICE Conditions of Contract, 6th Edition, January 1991, although the 5th Edition, June 1973 (revised January 1991) is still often used
— Civil Engineering Specification for the Water Industry, 4th Edition or Department of Transport Specification for Road and Bridge Works, 5th edition. Both of these may need additions and/or amendments for particular situations and materials associated with marine works, or
— Civil Engineering Standard Method of Measurement, 3rd edition, published by the Institution of Civil Engineers.

8. Practicalities of coastal defence construction

Construction in the marine environment presents a range of problems that must be addressed by client, designer and builder. The division of these roles is now often not so clear as in the past when responsibilities were separated, usually across three different organizations. Variants of the traditional forms of contractual arrangement now being employed for coastal defence schemes include the New Engineering Contract (NEC), 'Design, Build, Finance and Operate (DBFO)' and 'Public/Private Partnership (PPP)' arrangements. The main aim of these new arrangements is to ensure that risks are placed with those in the best position to manage them, thus reducing the likelihood and cost of contract disputes.

Whatever the contractual arrangements, however, there is a need to identify the division of responsibilities and risks before construction starts. Methods for managing the works should be clearly set out in the contract, as this can be a significant factor in the allocation of risk and the avoidance of later disputes. Bad weather can affect the coastline of the UK at any time of year, with the risk of delay or damage. Deciding at the tender stage on how these risks, and the potential financial losses, should be shared between the client and the contractor is also very important. Partnering arrangements help to facilitate the sharing of risk.

The designer's task is to produce a solution that is technically sound, cost effective and that can be built without undue difficulty or danger. This should be based upon techniques that can be practically achieved within the marine environment, within the specified time frame. Simplicity of design is often the key to a successful project. In the remainder of this chapter, numerous examples are given of situations where the designer needs to foresee and avoid practical problems that may occur in building a coastal defence at a particular site. However, other unexpected difficulties may arise, necessitating co-operation between the designer and the contractor to produce solutions. Some problems may be better dealt with by re-designing elements of the scheme rather than making major alterations to the proposed method of construction. This chapter of the report, therefore, is as relevant to the designer of coastal defences as to those building them.

Practical translation of the design into the completed scheme should be achieved without adverse construction-related effects on the stability of the completed structure, on its long-term performance or on the surrounding environment. This will require the appointment of a contractor experienced in marine works, and continuing supervision by representatives of the client or designer. The quality of both the supervision and the capability of the contractors are both crucially important if a coastal defence scheme is to be installed successfully and safely. Note that some of the new forms of contract, introduced above, will alter the normal supervisory arrangements; nevertheless the continued involvement of client, designer and contractor will still be beneficial to the success of a coastal defence scheme.

Clients, designers and contractors all have responsibilities for the safety of those involved in the construction and any subsequent maintenance, modification and repair of coastal defence works. Such works are specifically mentioned (as 'sea defence works') as 'Structures' in the Construction (Design and Management) Regulations introduced in the UK in 1994. Further discussion of this important aspect of the consideration, design, construction and subsequent management of coastal defence structures is presented in Section 8.7 of this guide.

The following outlines some of the special factors that need to be taken into account when building coastal defences, over and above the normal considerations for any major construction project.

8.1 Access and delivery/storage of materials

8.1.1 Access to the site

Access to and from the site of a coastal defence scheme is often a significant factor in the safe and efficient construction of a coastal defence scheme. Many sites will have either steep slopes or cliffs, or low-lying, soft ground on the landwards side, and water of variable depth to seawards. Cliffs or high seawalls may cause significant problems for the delivery of plant or bulky materials, see Figure 22. This may require the design of either a permanent access, or alternatively temporary works such as cranes or hoists to access the works. Similarly, access to the site across low-lying areas of poor ground may require construction of a temporary access and a careful assessment of the ground conditions. Further problems may arise where there are coastal roads, railways, promenades, footpaths or the like along the coastline just behind the site; as well as limiting access, it may be necessary to preserve public access during the construction period.

8.1.2 Access along the site

Arranging good access along a construction area, and finding adequate space for the safe storage of materials, are often problems as sites are typically long and narrow. The foreshore may be too soft or rocky to allow passage of plant, which will often be further restricted by high tides. Examples of expensive plant becoming cut off by a rising tide and immersed in seawater are recorded frequently around the UK (see Figure 23). Structures such as groynes or piers can also restrict access along a coastal frontage, and it may be impossible or damaging to remove them even temporarily. Because of these problems, it may be preferable to incorporate an access route into the design of the permanent coastal defences, for use during both the initial construction and subsequent maintenance of the scheme.

Access routes to a construction site may also have to be chosen carefully to avoid environmental damage. Such routes would typically have to be clearly marked and adhered to, in order to protect sensitive areas of the seabed, inter-tidal zone, beaches, dunes and the like. Similar considerations apply to the choice of areas used to store materials and equipment.

If available within a reasonable distance of the site, delivery of materials to the site by road can be cheaper than by sea. However, road deliveries can lead to traffic

Figure 22   Difficult plant access over seawall

Figure 23   Crane stranded at high tide

congestion and other problems, especially in urban areas and seaside resorts. Where materials have to be transported over large distances, on roads that are already congested or may be damaged by heavy cargoes, the option of delivery by sea needs to be considered carefully. This is particularly so with bulk materials such as rock armour, beach recharge, and earth-fill. The advantages may include a lower risk of accidents, less noise and pollution, and overall may be preferable from the viewpoint of 'sustainability'. However, it is also necessary to consider the possible adverse effects of such deliveries, for example on fishing, on navigation, and on marine life. Particular care will be needed when the inter-tidal zone, or offshore seabed, are specially designated under the Habitats Directive, e.g. SPA or SAC sites. Where these materials are sourced on land, adverse environmental effects may also occur along routes to and from the quayside from where they are shipped.

Access from the sea may also be difficult due to the tidal range, geometry and composition of the foreshore. Near-shore channels may result in fast flows that make mooring of large floating plant difficult; near-shore reefs may make the approach to the shoreline hazardous. The tidal range, geometry and composition of the seabed may limit the type of plant that is suitable for delivery.

Delivery of materials by sea may take several forms. In areas where the tidal range is large, options include bottom or side dumping of rock or beach recharge materials from barges, or beaching delivery vessels on the seabed at high water. The placed materials can then be recovered during subsequent low water periods. Beaching of barges, however, requires a suitable foreshore, free from hard rock or other obstructions. Where the tidal range is small, the construction of a temporary jetty for unloading may be the most appropriate method. This may be particularly suitable where the foreshore is steep, so only a short jetty is needed to reach sufficiently deep water for the draft of delivery vessels (see Figure 24).

Supply of dredged material by pipeline is a fast, efficient method for delivery of beach recharge material for large-scale projects. High mobilization costs make this option less attractive for smaller projects, typically less than 100 000 m^3, when road delivery may be cheaper. The size of dredger, grading of material and distance to the shoreline

Figure 24   Delivery of rock to temporary jetty

must be carefully considered due to limits on the pumping distance. Barge delivery by bottom-dumping for low water retrieval, or pumping from a dredger directly onto a beach (the rainbow method) can be more efficient on small-scale projects.

All these methods of delivery of materials by sea can be affected by waves or tidal currents. For example, swell waves greater than a metre high are likely to prevent the safe delivery of rock by barge, or connecting a dredger to a floating pipeline. Also, the limited availability of floating plant such as dredgers and large rock barges can lead to problems of mobilization and hence long 'lead-in times' for the project.

8.2 Tidal restrictions

The time available for construction during the tidal cycle is often the largest constraint on a construction timetable, and this is an important difference between the construction of coastal defences and of inland or offshore engineering projects. Access, and the time available for working 'in the dry', is restricted by the changing water levels relative to the toe and crest levels of the defences, and by the foreshore type and shape. The use of floating plant may also be possible only at certain stages of the tidal cycle, for example because of strong currents or the need for a sufficient water depth close inshore to avoid grounding.

Predicted tidal conditions may be affected by surges or wave conditions, which can increase but more normally reduce the length of the working day. In some circumstances, a combination of neap tides and/or bad weather may result in no activity being possible for several weeks. Certain phases of work may have to be completed within a single tidal cycle and partially completed sections of work may have to be removed before work can recommence. Designers should consider the limitations that the tidal 'window' will have on both quantity and quality of construction to ensure that acceptable levels of partial completion can be achieved within a tidal cycle. Concrete seawalls present the most complicated requirements for phased and partial construction; simplification of design details can therefore make significant differences to the cost and effectiveness of the construction phase.

Excavation of the foundation and toe detail of structures can cause significant problems, depending upon ground conditions. When the structure requires an excavation in hard rock, this can often be allowed to remain open between tidal cycles. Excavations in sand and gravel, however, may require to be covered in order to prevent them being rapidly infilled. At certain sites, the toe of a structure may be below the lowest tidal level and special temporary works must be put in place to allow safe excavation, pouring concrete and underwater construction. Temporary structures such as cofferdams can be built but these are often extremely expensive for linear defences and their construction may have a negative effect on the stability of the completed structure. The time frame available for construction of a foundation will affect the designer's choice of materials. The design and construction of concrete structures underwater requires special techniques that can result in significant costs.

The spring-neap tidal cycle presents both opportunities for and constraints on coastal defence construction. High water periods during spring tides are often favoured for delivery of materials by sea while low waters present opportunities for excavation of toe trenches and concreting at low levels. At any site, the times of high and low waters during the largest spring tides will be at roughly the same time of day throughout the year, at midday or midnight in some places, and early morning/early evening at others.

8.3 Seasonal and phased construction

8.3.1 Seasonal working

The various practical difficulties in building coastal defences can be increased or diminished depending on the time of year. For example, a delay of only a few weeks in starting construction, particularly just after the end of the summer holiday season, can mean that weather and wave conditions will have deteriorated significantly. This can affect both the rates of working and the safety of those involved in that work. Because of this, a number of aspects have to be considered during the planning of construction works, as described below.

In addition, the intended timing of the construction should be clearly stated in tender documents. It is important to consider the extra risks and hence costs of construction during periods when there is a risk of severe weather damaging or delaying work. Sharing or acceptance of such risks within a contract can result in lower tender prices.

8.3.1.1 Working conditions. In the UK, all coastal defences would be built during summer months if the efficient and timely completion of an engineering scheme was the only consideration. The rate of progress and quality of work is likely to be higher while the risk of downtime due to weather is considerably reduced, both factors leading to lower costs. However, construction activities in summer may be unwelcome because of the disruption they cause during the holiday season, particularly when works are planned for popular seaside resorts. The financial advantages of construction in good weather need to be carefully balanced against the potential disruption to the holiday season and hence to the local economy. It is worth making the point that, when construction take place in seaside towns, the works themselves are often of considerable interest to holidaymakers and local residents alike. Preventing public access to construction areas, especially beaches where access is not usually restricted, can be an additional problem to safe working. Where summer working is permitted, working hour restrictions are often imposed and strictly enforced. Activities that are usually carried out on a 24-hour basis may have to be curtailed, resulting in dramatic cost increases.

There are generally few technical problems affecting construction during the summer months. Sun and wind can have significant adverse effects on exposed areas of *in situ* concrete. Adequate measures to protect the concrete, or to combat effects caused by the rise in temperature of massive pours due to the heat of the hydration of cement, and subsequent shrinkage may be specified. The likelihood of higher beach levels during summer months can also increase the quantity of excavation required for toe and foundation details.

During the winter, the reduced hours of daylight can reduce the working day, over and above the limiting effects of tides. In addition, stormy weather and the frequent low atmospheric pressure can mean that the useful working time on the lower part of an inter-tidal beach is less than might be expected based on the published tide-tables. Normal 'land-based' construction problems such as the effects of low temperatures, for example on concreting, further compound the problem of winter working in the marine environment

8.3.1.2 Delivery of materials. The practicality of delivering bulky materials will vary with the time of the year. Delivery by sea during winter months will run an increased risk of delays and dangers, with a corresponding reduction in progress, due to the greater likelihood of stormy weather. Hence, for each site, the difficulties of safe navigation, mooring and unloading vessels in shallow water should be carefully evaluated for different times of the year. Information on the meteorological and hydrodynamic conditions likely to occur should be combined with knowledge and experience of the 'threshold' limits, e.g. current speeds and wave conditions, beyond which it is not safe to work.

Conversely, delivery by road during the summer holiday season, usually between April and September, can also be a problem, with attendant increased risks of accidents and delays.

8.3.1.3 Environmental effects. Carrying out construction works at a suitable time of year can reduce their adverse effects on the environment. For example, works in estuaries are likely, in some areas, to be more disruptive between late autumn and early spring, when there may be important numbers of migrating or over-wintering birds. In other areas, it may be necessary to avoid disturbance to spawning or migrating fish, or to nesting birds. The environmental appraisal or impact assessment for a coastal defence scheme should have identified these possible problems and indicated any appropriate mitigation measures, including time periods appropriate to the works being carried out (see Section 6.3).

8.3.1.4 Safety. Seasonal effects on the safety of both the construction workers and the public should be considered. Where possible, works should be completed in short segments to maximize the space available to the public during the construction phases that take place during the summer months. Generally, problems in excluding the public, and especially children, from dangerous areas are greater during the holiday season.

In winter months, the dangers to construction workers will clearly be greater. Lower water temperatures, stronger winds and larger waves, and factors such as ice and reduced visibility all make accidents more likely, and potentially more serious. Seasonal effects should therefore be identified in the overall safety plan for the works prepared under the CDM regulations (see Section 8.7).

8.3.1.5 Damage to part-completed works. There is always a risk of damage to partially completed work, since bad weather conditions can occur at any time of the year in the UK. Such risks, however, are clearly much higher during the winter and additional safety measures to protect works may be necessary. This may be particularly important during the construction of rock structures that have small underlayer material beneath the armour stone. Provision of stockpiles of additional materials to carry out short-term emergency repairs is recommended. Such stockpiles, and parking areas for plant, may also have to be relocated to safer areas in the winter, to avoid possible damage or loss caused by high seas.

8.3.2 Phased construction

Where possible, the designer should ensure that the various stages of the construction of a coastal defence can be completed without significant interruption and delay, and without affecting the overall integrity of the works. The methods of working and sequence of construction necessary to ensure good performance during and following construction of the scheme should be specified. For example, the construction of hard structures such as seawalls and groynes will generally best be completed before a recharge, to avoid double handling of the beach materials.

Because working in the inter-tidal zone is generally more constrained than above high water, staged construction allowing completion of the lower parts of a structure may allow faster progress than fully completing short sections of the defences. However, the designer may need to impose limits on the construction sequence to ensure the integrity of the works under these circumstances.

Phased construction of coastal defences may be needed for a variety of reasons including, seasonal restrictions, cash flow and to observe the performance of a pilot scheme. Large-scale projects may take several working seasons to complete, particularly if construction work is permitted only during part of a year. However, such an approach to construction will often create a number of problems, and may significantly increase costs, perhaps to an unacceptable extent.

First, special planning of the construction phases will be necessary. Vulnerable sections of the works may require additional temporary protection measures to prevent damage prior to completion of the scheme. If there are some months between phases, then plant may have to be de-mobilized and mobilized again, incurring further costs and the potential for delays. There could also be increased risk to adjacent uncompleted sections due to effects from completed works. Further 'overhead' contract costs may arise dealing with conflicts at boundaries of the different phases of a scheme, and it is best to avoid breaking down contracts into more elements than necessary to avoid these problems.

8.4 Planning and environmental considerations

A coastal defence scheme will usually have been submitted for, and received, planning approval and other consents prior to the construction phase (see Chapter 7). However, additional licences and permissions may be needed once the contractor has been appointed. For example, the successful tenderer may have proposed methods for delivery or building that were not anticipated by the designer, and which require consents from local or national government bodies. Examples may include consents for the disposal of material at sea (e.g. for a beach recharge scheme, to protect the environment against pollution), or for installing temporary works off the coastline that might be an obstruction to navigation or fishing. Construction programmes should allow sufficient time to obtain such additional consents, especially if it seems likely that environmental effects may be deemed sufficient to require a formal assessment before such consents were obtained.

The construction of a coastal defence scheme may well have been identified as having the potential for causing adverse effects on the environment. The execution of such works should therefore be carried out with due regard to the findings and recommendations of the environmental appraisal or impact assessment (see Section 6.3), and any conditions attached to any licences and consents, for example planning permission. For example, to maximize productivity it is often planned to work two tidal shifts each day during certain stages of building a coastal defence. Certain activities, such as dredging and rock delivery regularly take place on a 24-hour basis. However, this can result in unacceptable noise levels and disturbance. If construction outside normal working hours is unacceptable the designer and contractor may need to consider alternative types of construction or phasing of the work, and this could have significant cost implications.

Other conditions attaching to consents, or recommendations from the Environmental Statement, may suggest:

— methods of working to mitigate or avoid damage
— materials selection based on environmental criteria
— arrangements for monitoring and supervision of construction activities, and
— liaison, for example with conservation organizations.

Liaison arrangements with the local community, and regional or national conservation organizations, are important and efforts should be made to establish good working relationships as soon as possible. These may include meetings to discuss the progress of the works, and any effects on the local community, on fishing activities, on the local ecology and other aspects such as archaeology. Early identification of concerns, and a willingness to discuss these, may avoid disputes that could cause delays in completing the scheme, and hence unnecessary expense.

8.5 Construction plant and methods

The suitability and availability of plant is an important factor in the efficiency of building coastal defences. This issue thus needs to be taken into account both during the design stage and when planning the construction programme. Long sloping structures may cause problems particularly if armoured with very large rock, when access from the toe or crest is restricted. The combination of reach, weight and speed of operation of the plant needs to be carefully balanced with the choice and availability of the construction materials.

Ground conditions may present practical difficulties during construction, limiting access to heavy plant, or limiting construction methods because of the low shear strength of the ground. This, for example, may limit the depth of a beach recharge or may mean that it has to be constructed in layers. If the sand or gravel used for the recharge is to be pumped onshore, suitable locations must be found for the drainage of large volumes of pumping water.

8.6 Measurement and detailing

Measurement of construction materials in the marine environment often presents problems, particularly when volume measurements are to be made. Measurement of beach recharge may take place either on the beach or in the hopper. There may however be significant losses during the construction process and payment in the hopper will not ensure the correct volume on the beach. Dynamic structures such as beaches must be measured soon after construction otherwise there will be a high risk of losses of material that are not measured.

The complex nature of rock armour construction, in placing the rocks to achieve the desired depth and permeability of the various layers as well as the design dimensions, makes measurements difficult. These are normally made either by measuring the weight of the rocks supplied, or the in- volume, perhaps converting this weight using a target density, established using a trial section or 'panel' of the scheme. This latter method is more difficult and a higher risk lies with the contractor in this respect. Payment by weight provides a number of advantages and is generally favoured by the contractor. This method provides greater flexibility in meeting the client's brief and in the construction of complex detail. Disputes may arise whichever method is used, however, and clarity in the contract regarding placement and measurement methods is important in this respect (see Latham et al., in press).

Simplicity of design detailing will also help in construction being carried out quickly and accurately. Often this means reducing the number of different grades of rock to a minimum. Trying to achieve complex geometry and detail using rock armour can present considerable difficulties. Intersections of complex slopes and straight parallel lines of armour are extremely difficult to achieve. Plane slopes achieved by use of blocky armour can also increase overtopping beyond that normally expected from rock armour. Balancing the stability requirements of layer thickness, placement density and grading can result in structures that may practically be impossible to build.

Tolerances stated should consider the size of materials in use. Similarly, realistic tolerances should be given for the dimensions of a beach recharge scheme, particularly when materials are placed in the active inter-tidal zone. Even modest wave action will rapidly re-shape a recharged beach, so that it is the total volume of sand or gravel placed that is the most important measure.

8.7 Construction risks

8.7.1 Financial risks

Construction within the marine environment is an activity with high risks. Bad weather can result in delays, with consequential financial losses. As noted earlier, the designer and client will have a number of opportunities to share such risks with the contractor, and this approach should result in lower tender prices. A common example would be the apportionment of losses arising from bad weather. Appropriate methods will be needed to measure adverse conditions, for example by installing a wave-rider buoy offshore from the site. The client may pay demurrage if conditions exceed a defined sea state for a greater than anticipated period. If better weather than expected prevails during the construction period, this would then also result in lower scheme costs overall. Specification of reasonable tolerances in the dimensions of a design, using equitable methods of measurement and simplicity of designs will all reduce financial risks further.

8.7.2 Health and safety issues

In addition to any financial risks, there are also clear dangers to construction workers and the public within and around the construction site. As noted in the introductory section of this Chapter, coastal defences fall under the provisions of the Construction (Design and Management) Regulations, Health and Safety Commission (1995). These place duties on all involved in the commissioning, design and construction of such works. Some of the most important aspects of these Regulations, in the context of building coastal defences, are briefly summarized below; further information can be found in Simm and Cruickshank (1998).

The designer will be required to provide a statement under these regulations that informs those tendering of the risks in building the defences that it has not been practical to eliminate during the design process. Consideration must also be given to the health and safety of those that may be engaged in maintenance operations after the coastal defences have been completed, together with people who might 'use' the scheme, for example, holidaymakers.

Under the tendering process, it is essential that the client ensures that any contractor placed on a short-list is competent to carry out the required work. Once a contractor is selected, it is then required under the same CDM regulations that the client will not allow any construction work to be started before an adequate health and safety plan has been prepared by that contractor. This plan will need to consider the safety of both the public and those engaged in the executing the works.

8.8 Construction supervision

The many potential difficulties that can arise when building a coastal defence scheme mean that high quality supervision of the construction is particularly important. This will include the supervision of both the contract and the safety aspects of the construction, although these two responsibilities may be carried out by different organizations. Sudden changes in weather conditions, and the common practice for working over tidal cycles, mean that supervision will need to be almost continuous during some stages of the construction timetable.

Close supervision will assist in resolving contract disputes, for example by timely consideration of variation orders in the light of changing circumstances and monitoring of works in progress. The supervisory staff will also have an important role in liaison with the public and other organizations, as described in Section 8.4, and if necessary arranging for specialist supervision from archaeologists or ecologists for certain aspects of the project.

9. Post-project monitoring, maintenance and evaluation

9.1 Introduction

As noted in earlier sections of this guide, the cost-effective management of any coastline, and its defences, is dependent upon a well-planned and long-term monitoring programme. A monitoring programme will help identify and understand developing problems along a coastline, and help in assessing the need for, and design of a possible coastal defence scheme. When such defences are likely to be built, it is often helpful to intensify the monitoring locally, to provide detailed information on conditions at the site. For example, prior to a beach recharge it is worth increasing the frequency of beach surveys so that the volume of the existing beach and the short-term variations in that volume can be established.

However, increased monitoring should then continue during and after the installation of any coastal defences, so that the performance and effects of the scheme can be assessed. In addition, no coastal defence can be expected to be 'maintenance-free'. As noted in Section 6.1.3, the operational life and durability of a defence depends on the management and maintenance strategy adopted. The maintenance works undertaken, in turn, will be based on the monitoring of the defences and the adjacent coastline.

It should be realized, however, that monitoring the coastline, and its defences, can be an expensive task. It must therefore be carefully matched to the required objectives of the defences and to the value of the assets protected. The frequency and extent of the monitoring carried out, and the maintenance of defences, should both be regularly reviewed to optimize the management of the coastline.

While some monitoring of coastal defences is often carried out as a matter of course, it has been increasingly common in recent years to carry out a formal assessment of a scheme, known as a 'post-project evaluation'. Such assessments are regarded as important, at least partly because this is an area still inadequately covered in construction codes and European regulations. Therefore, the final section of this chapter describes such post-project evaluations.

This chapter sets out suggestions for a number of post-project activities, divided into the following main categories:

— construction evaluation

— monitoring the condition of the defences
— maintenance of the defences
— performance evaluation (including hydrodynamic conditions experienced)
— interaction of the defence with beaches/shoreline
— assessing other environmental effects.

9.2 Construction evaluation

Ideally, all coastal defence schemes should be subject to a 'construction evaluation' during which feedback on the conduct of the construction phase is obtained from all parties. This should include obtaining views from the project manager or another representative of the client, from the designer, from the 'builder', i.e. the engineering contractors, and from any other parties to the contract. Where appropriate it should also seek responses from third parties such as landowners, conservation organizations, other interested parties and the public.

The purpose of these consultations will be to bring together experience from the conduct of the works and disseminate lessons which should be taken into account in any future projects, at the same site or elsewhere. In some circumstances, where installing a defence scheme extends over a long period, it may also be valuable to start such evaluations during the works programme. This could lead to changing construction methods or practices if better ones could be employed, for example causing less damage to the environment or reducing risks to the contractors or the public.

The construction evaluation is also the starting point for post-project monitoring. Complete 'as-built' survey records of any defences are important for evaluation of any subsequent failures and can be invaluable when planning any upgrading or rebuilding works later in the life of the defences. Provision should also be made to retain accessible records of the philosophy and assumptions behind the design. This knowledge will then not be lost because of changes of personnel and is available to those carrying out maintenance or management activities during the life of the structure.

9.3 Monitoring the condition of defences

The condition of all elements of a defence scheme should be monitored regularly. This applies equally well to beaches in front of any structures as well as the structures themselves (see Figure 25) since beach levels can often affect both the functional performance and the structural integrity of the defences.

The main purpose of this monitoring will be to ensure that early warning is available to identify any maintenance requirements. However, the data will be important in the assessment of the scheme performance, and any post-project evaluation. Inspection of mechanical elements or concrete structures should be carried out routinely, for example at the beginning and/or end of the winter and after severe storms where damage might have occurred. Such inspections are usually carried out by visual inspection, perhaps with photographs, during a 'walk over' survey. Where this reveals significant changes in defences, then more detailed survey methods may be warranted.

Innovative methods may be required to monitor the condition of structures such as rock revetments or breakwaters. For these, it will be important to monitor any armour displacement or potential instability when assessing the need for, and cost of, maintenance.

Figure 25   Surveying of coastal defence structures

Monitoring will be an important element of all beach management schemes since in the original design it will usually be appropriate to set critical levels, which will probably be seasonally dependent, to trigger management intervention. However, long term monitoring has a wider function in relation to the performance of a beach management scheme. Without detailed records of changes in beach morphology and its response to different events, it is impossible to assess the scheme's effectiveness.

Whilst local beach surveys can be used to monitor individual scheme performance, larger scale surveys on a coastal cell or regional basis will be necessary to assess the wider impacts of any works. As a guide it is probably desirable to take beach cross-sections at about one-kilometre intervals at least twice per year (in summer and winter) and extend these seawards to cover as much of the active beach as possible. For stretches of the shoreline where the functional efficiency of a defence is crucially dependent on beach levels, surveying both before and immediately after storm events can be valuable.

In complex areas, it may well be necessary to increase the density of surveying, perhaps abandoning the use of simple cross-sections and taking levels over a grid to provide a three-dimensional 'surface elevation model' of the beach surface. However, careful thought should be given, in advance, about the information needed and how to analyse the surveys to provide this.

The level of the beach at it crest is the most important single parameter in determining the performance of a coastal defence. Since upper beach levels are generally lowest in winter (e.g. between December and February), this is the most important time to survey a beach. Surveys at other times in the year, for example in mid summer (June–August) will give information on seasonal variations, and can be extended lower down the beach profile with less difficulty. Because of this, they are more useful for calculating the changing volumes of beach material.

Beach surveys should, at least occasionally, be extended underwater to provide information on changes on the nearshore seabed. The use of GPS/RTK (real-time kinematic) techniques have simplified and improved hydrographic surveying. Even so, it is always useful to arrange for an 'overlap' between conventional beach surveys (at low water) and bathymetric surveying (at high water) of the nearshore seabed, to help reduce errors in the soundings. It is unusual for such surveys to be carried out as frequently as once a year, except perhaps when rapid changes in the nearshore seabed are suspected.

For regional scale monitoring, consideration should be given to the use of advanced survey techniques and methods of remote sensing such as low level aerial photography and LIDAR. These can be used to rapidly acquire a large amount of data for wider areas, including low-lying land behind coastal defences. They may be particularly useful for areas where conventional surveying is awkward or dangerous, for example inter-tidal mudflats and saltmarshes, cliffs and coastal slopes.

9.4 Maintenance

Maintenance should be considered as an integral part of the design process: the design life of a structure should be considered by reference to potential life cycle maintenance costs. No coastal defences are maintenance free, although costs can be very low in some cases. A generic maintenance programme cannot be pre-scribed for each structure type, as materials and environmental conditions vary with location.

Concrete structures rarely require a high maintenance commitment, although re-facing of reinforced structures may sometimes be required in aggressive environments charged with abrasive materials. Consideration should be given to monitoring the rate of wear of concrete and cover of reinforcing.

Rock structure maintenance costs can vary considerably, depending on the durability of materials, whether the structure is designed for static or dynamic stability and the environmental conditions. Use of low-grade rock may result in rapid abrasion or breakage of armourstone, leading to significant structural damage. A broad-brush guideline average sum of 1% of capital cost per annum is suggested for rock structures although maintenance should not usually be required every year. This is based on statically stable structures armoured with high-grade materials. Rock structures may need 'topping up' within a few years of construction due to settlement, but generally only require significant levels of maintenance following severe storm events.

Cyclic maintenance is often required on timber structures, as each of the elements degrades at different rates, creating weak links. Effective planning and replacement of less durable elements, such as bolts in a shingle charged environment, can reduce costly replacement of timbers if effected in a timely manner. Maintenance commitments can vary greatly, depending on the environment, from full replacement of structures within a period of five years to minimal maintenance over 25 years. Periodic routine inspections can identify local life cycle trends of each structure element, which enables effective site specific planning of low cost maintenance.

Coastal defences structures of low capital cost can require expensive and frequent maintenance (see Figure 26) and even then may only have a limited service life.

Figure 26   Maintenance of gabion revetment

Beach recharge schemes often have a low capital cost, but usually require a high level of subsequent maintenance in terms of either recycling (see Figure 27) or interim recharge. The maintenance programme can often be fine tuned with the aid of a monitoring programme and simple predictive models of profile response and long-shore transport, which can be used to establish alarm conditions. Costly emergency plant mobilization and importation of local material at premium rates following storm damage can often be avoided if proactive planned beach maintenance is carried out. Consideration needs to be given to optimization of interim recharge by reference to the flooding or erosion risks to be managed, to the mobilization costs, to the timing of works, and the relative costs of sea delivery and supply.

All maintenance records should be collated and fed back into local beach management and shoreline management plans, to allow these strategic planning documents to be updated.

9.5 Evaluation of defence performance

A crucial part of any project monitoring is the assessment of the functional performance of a defence. The scope of the monitoring of functional performance will depend primarily on the objectives determined for the original scheme. For example, if the objective is to limit flooding or disruption through overtopping by wave action then steps should be taken to record wave activity during storm events. If flooding

Figure 27   Beach recycling following beach recharge

occurs, records of levels and estimation of flows should be made as soon as possible after the event. Where the defence depends on the operation of structural elements, such as surge barriers, it is important that details such as the frequency of operation are recorded. Any deficiencies in either physical operation or supporting operations such as the availability of adequate warnings should also be recorded.

In addition to monitoring the performance of a defence scheme, it is very important to keep records of the 'environmental' conditions, i.e. waves, tidal levels and currents to which the scheme is exposed. Archiving of wind, wave and tidal data will enable evaluators to compare the actual performance of the scheme against that anticipated during the original design. This monitoring will also show whether the wave and tide conditions it has experienced are as expected, and as used in the design of the defences. Predicted climate changes resulting from global warming may mean that this may become more important in future years. Information on both the functional performance of a defence, and of the environmental conditions it has experienced, will be important in considering any modification or redesign of the scheme, and to improve the design of similar schemes elsewhere.

Formal performance evaluations should ideally be carried out at approximately five-year intervals from initial commissioning of any project.

9.6 Environmental monitoring

Further monitoring should be directed to measurement of achievement of the original environmental objectives of the scheme so that actual changes can be compared with those predicted in the Environmental Impact Assessment. This may be especially important if there were uncertainties in the evaluation of the possible effects of a particular scheme. However, it will also be desirable for environmental monitoring to include a number of general indicators so that unexpected effects, whether positive or negative, can be identified.

9.7 Post-project evaluations

The purpose of carrying out post-project evaluations is to assess the effectiveness of the investment made in coastal defences and to ensure that lessons are learnt for the execution of future works. The data required for carrying out an evaluation should also be valuable in the proper planning of subsequent maintenance and management activities. Although post-project evaluations are carried out for individual schemes, they can be aggregated to provide a wider regional or national overview of coastal defence works, to determine the overall effectiveness of the investments made.

Clearly, the detail and extent of all evaluations should be appropriate to the scale of the original projects, taking account of the complexity of the original objectives. Whilst it is desirable that evaluations are carried out by those outside the original project team, and a proportion should be undertaken by independent third parties, this would not be a justifiable requirement for all evaluations.

Ideally, the findings of all evaluations should be made available as widely as possible though it is recognized that this may have to be handled with some sensitivity. However, the principle should be that the lessons from each project are disseminated effectively to others in the industry so that there is an ongoing accumulation of knowledge and expertise.

A post-project evaluation will consist of a programme of data collection followed by analysis, largely comparing actual conditions and results against those anticipated during the planning and design of the scheme. All such evaluations should consider the technical, financial and environmental aspects of the project.

9.8 Data storage, sharing and future use

As noted earlier in this guide, monitoring of the coastline, and its processes, whether locally or at a regional (e.g. coastal cell) level is very valuable when:

— updating and reviewing strategic plans for shoreline management and coastal defences
— understanding the mechanisms and rates of shoreline change
— assessing the need for, and the possible types of, coastal defences, and
— providing information for use in the design of defences.

Ideally, such monitoring should have been started well in advance of the consideration of coastal defences, so that much of the information needed to assess alternative options (see Chapter 5) is available at that time. However, such monitoring is often not started until the problems of erosion or flooding have sharpened interest in coastal defences. Wherever possible, once collection of information on the coast has been started it should be continued with a view to aiding evaluation of the success of schemes and assisting in future decision making.

This data may be useful in the same general area or elsewhere at similar sites. The usefulness of any information can be considerably improved if early consideration is given to the analysis, presentation, storage, dissemination and sharing of that information. Millard and Sayers (2000) discuss these topics in detail in a research report produced by CIRIA and this should be consulted as part of the planning process for any coastal data collection programme.

Bibliography

Allen, R. T. L. (ed.) (1998) *Concrete in Coastal Structures*. Thomas Telford, London.

British Trust for Conservation Volunteers (1996) *Sand Dunes – A Practical Handbook*. British Trust for Conservation Volunteers, Wallingford, Oxfordshire.

Bromhead, E. N. (1986) *The Stability of Slopes*. Surrey University Press, Guildford.

Brunsden, D. and Prior, D. B. (1984) *Slope Instability (Landscape Systems, a Series in Geomorphology)*. John Wiley, Chichester.

Burt, T. N. and Rees, A. (eds) (2001) *Guidelines for the Assessment and Planning of Estuarine Barrages*. Thomas Telford, London.

Campbell, N. P., MacLeod, D. C. and Swart, D. H. (1985) Bypassing and beach nourishment scheme at Durban. *26th International Navigation Congress*, Section II, Subject 3, Brussels, 7–18.

CIRIA (1996) *Beach Management Manual*. Construction Industry Research and Information Association, Report 153.

CIRIA/CUR (1991) *Manual on the Use of Rock in Coastal and Shoreline Engineering*. CIRIA Special Publication 83/CUR Report 154.

Commission of the European Communities (1992) Integrated management of the coastal areas of the European Community. *Conference of the Peripheral Maritime Regions*.

Commission of the European Communities (1995) Communication from the Commission to the Council and the European Parliament on the integrated management of coastal zones. November.

Coughlan, P. M. and Robinson, D. A. (1990) The Gold Coast Seaway, Queensland, Australia. *Shore & Beach* **58**, 9–16.

Council for Nature Conservation and the Countryside (1993) Coastal zone management policy for Northern Ireland.

Council for Nature Conservation and the Countryside (1995) *Delivering Coastal Zone Management in Northern Ireland*. Environment Service, Belfast.

Davison, A. T., Nicholls, R. J. and Leatherman, S. P. (1992) Beach nourishment as a coastal management tool: An annotated bibliography on developments associated with the artificial nourishment of beaches. *Journal of Coastal Research* **8**, 984–1022.

Delft Hydraulics Laboratory (1987) *Manual on Artificial Beach Nourishment*. Report 130.

Department of Energy (1989) *Offshore Installations: Guidance on Design and Construction. Part II, Meteorological and Oceanographic Design Parameters*. Report PEA/68/35/1.

Department of the Environment (1995) *Policy Guidelines for the Coast – PPG20*. Publication 95CCG 218, November 1995, HMSO, London

Department of the Environment (1996) *Coastal Zone Management – Towards Best Practice*. Report prepared by Nicholas Pearson Associates, October.

Dixon, M. J. and Tawn, J. A. (1997) *Spatial Analyses for the UK Coast*. Proudman Oceanographic Laboratory, Internal Document No 112, Natural Environment Research Council.

Draper, L. (1991) *Wave Climate Atlas of the British Isles*. Department of Energy: Offshore Technology Report OTH89 903, HMSO, London.

Environment Agency (1999) *Overtopping of Seawalls – Design and Assessment Manual*. EA R&D Technical Report W178, Research Contractor; HR Wallingford Ltd, Oxon.

Environment Agency (Carpenter, K. E.) (1996) *Maintenance and Enhancement of Saltmarshes.* Report for NRA (R&D Note 473), Research Contractor; HR Wallingford Ltd, Oxon.

Environment Service, Belfast (1995) *Delivering Coastal Zone Management in Northern Ireland – A Consultation Paper.* Published on behalf of government in Northern Ireland.

Fiorentino, A., Franco, L. and Noli, A. (1985) Sand bypassing plant at Viareggio (Italy). *Australasian Conference on Coastal and Ocean Engineering*, Christchurch, New Zealand.

Fleming, C. A. (1990) *Guide to the use of Groynes in Coastal Engineering.* Construction Industry Research and Information Association (CIRIA), Report 119.

Fletcher, C. A., Stevenson, J. R. and Dearnaley, M. P. (2001) *The Beneficial Use of Muddy Dredged Material.* HR Report SR 579, HR Wallingford Ltd, Oxon. Funded by DEFRA FCD, April 2001.

Harford, C. M. (1998). *A Catalogue of Instrumentally Measured Wave Data Around the Coast of England and Wales.* Report TR 51, HR Wallingford, Oxon.

Health & Safety Commission (1995) *Managing Construction for Health and Safety. Construction Design and Management) Regulations 1994 – Approved Code of Practice.* Publication L54, HSE Books, London.

Hsu, J. R. C., Silvester, R. and Xia, Y. M. (1989). Generalities on static equilibrium bays. *Coastal Engineering* **12**, 353–369.

Hutchinson, J. N. (2001). Reading the ground: morphology and geology in site appraisal (fourth Glossop lecture), *Quarterly Journal of Engineering Geology and Hydrogeology* **34**, 7–50.

Jones, C. P. and Mehta, A. J. (1980) Inlet sand bypassing systems in Florida. *Shore & Beach* **48**, 25–34.

Latham, J.-P., Newberry, S. D., Mannion, M., Simm, J. and Stewart, T. (in press) The void porosity of rock armour in coastal structures with reference to measurement and payment issues. *Proceedings of the Institution of Civil Engineers, Water, Maritime & Energy*, Paper 2479.

Lee, E. M. and Clark, A. R. (in press) *Investigation and Management for Soft Rock Cliffs I.* Thomas Telford, London.

McConnell, K. (1998) *Revetment Systems Against Wave Attack – A Design Manual.* Thomas Telford, London.

Millard, T. K. and Sayers, P. B. (2000) Maximising the Use and Exchange of Coastal Data – A Guide to Best Practice. Construction Industry Research and Information Association (CIRIA) Publication, C541.

Ministry of Agriculture, Fisheries and Food (1993) *Flood and Coastal Defence. Project Appraisal Guidance Notes.* Publication PB1214, HMSO, London.

Ministry of Agriculture, Fisheries and Food (1999) *Flood and Coastal Defence Project Appraisal Guidance: Economic Appraisal.* FCDPAG3, Publication PB 4650, HMSO, London.

Ministry of Agriculture, Fisheries and Food (2000) *Flood and Coastal Defence Project Appraisal Guidance: Approaches to Risk.* FCDPAG4, Publication PB 4907, HMSO, London.

Ministry of Agriculture, Fisheries and Food (2000) *Flood and Coastal Defence Project Appraisal Guidance: Environmental Appraisal.* FCDPAG5, Publication PB 4915, HMSO, London.

Ministry of Agriculture, Fisheries and Food (2001) *Flood and Coastal Defence Project Appraisal Guidance: Overview.* FCDPAG1, HMSO, London.

Ministry of Agriculture, Fisheries and Food (2001) *Flood and Coastal Defence Project Appraisal Guidance: Strategic Planning and Appraisal.* FCDPAG2, HMSO, London.

Ministry of Agriculture, Fisheries and Food and the Welsh Office (1993) *Strategy for Flood and Coastal Defence in England and Wales.* Publication PB1471, HMSO, London.

Ministry of Agriculture, Fisheries and Food, Welsh Office, Association of District Councils, English Nature and National Rivers Authority (1995) *Shoreline Management Plans. A Guide for Coastal Defence Authorities.* Publication PB2197, HMSO, London.

National Assembly for Wales (1999) *The Coast and Inshore Waters of Wales: An Inheritance Document*, Cardiff, pp. 16.

Open University (1997) *Waves, Tides and Shallow-water Processes.* Prepared by an Open University Course Team, Butterworth Heinemann, Oxford.

Owen, M. W., Hawkes, P. J., Tawn, J. and Bortot, P. (1997) The joint probability of waves and water levels: A rigorous but practical new approach. *Proceedings of 32nd MAFF Conference of River and Coastal Engineers*, Keele University.

Parker, D. J., Green, C. H. and Thompson, P. M. (1987) *Urban Flood Protection Benefits: A Project Appraisal Guide (the Red Manual).* Gower Technical Press, Aldershot.

Penning-Rowsell, E. C., Green, C. H., Thompson, P. M., Coker, A. M., Tunstall, S. M., Richards, C. and Parker, D. J. (1992) *The Economics of Coastal Management: A Manual of Benefits Assessment Techniques* (the Yellow Manual). Belhaven Press, London.

Pugh, D. T. (1991) *Tides, Surges and Mean Sea-level. A Handbook for Engineers and Scientists*. John Wiley, Chichester.

Ranwell, D. S. and Boar, R. (1986) *Coastal Dune Management Guide*. Institute of Terrestrial Ecology, Natural Environment Research Council.

Rijkswaterstaat (1985) *The Use of Asphalt in Hydraulic Engineering*. Technical Advisory Committee on Water Defences, Communication no. 37, The Hague.

Sayers, P. B. and Simm, J. D. (2001) *Residual Life: Its Assessment and Importance in Terms of Coastal Management and Benefit Analysis*. HR Wallingford Report SR 499.

Scottish Natural Heritage (2000) *A Guide to Managing Coastal Erosion in Beach/Dune Systems*. Scottish Natural Heritage, Edinburgh.

Scottish Office (1996) *Scotland's Coasts A Discussion Paper*. HMSO, London.

Simm, J. D. and Cruickshank, I. C. (1998) *Construction Risk in Coastal Engineering*. Thomas Telford, London.

Sorensen, R. M. (1993) *Basic Wave Mechanics for Coastal and Ocean Engineers*. John Wiley, Chichester.

Thomas, R. S. and Hall, B. (1992) *Seawall Design*. Construction Industry Research and Information Association Construction Industry Research and Information Association (CIRIA)/Butterworths, London.

United Kingdom Climate Change Impacts Review Group (1996) *Review of the Potential Effects of Climate Change in the United Kingdom – Second Report*. HMSO, London.

Wakeling, H. L., Cox N. J. and others (1983) A study of littoral drift at Paradip, India. *International Conference on Coastal and Port Engineering in Developing Countries*, Colombo, Sri Lanka, Proceedings **2**, 1192–1206.

Welsh Office (1998) *Technical Advice Note (TAN) 14, Coastal Planning*. Cardiff.

World Commission on Environment and Development (1987) *Our Common Future*. Oxford University Press, Oxford.